"When you know better you do better."
– *Maya Angelou*

"David has done it again. More than a sequel, this book provides fresh insight into why many leaders fail—and how they can change course. 'The Se7en Deadly Sins of Leadership' are especially poignant. Every leader should have the courage to face bad habits and the conviction to change them. David shows how in this thought-provoking book."

　　— *Carolyn Rose, Director, Global Internal Communications, Rockwell Automation*

"David Grossman is a savvy, experienced, intuitive partner. He has an unusual ability to quickly divine your organization's culture—both on and below the surface—and diagnose what's needed to make it work more effectively. Grossman's combination of instinctual perception and practical advice is rare. Whether you're new to your organization or a veteran, whether you're driving change or honing what you have, David Grossman's insight will accelerate your efforts. His understanding of the art of communication and what makes an organization come alive as a result of effective communication from the top has been a tremendous help as we have shaped our company's culture around a new management team."

　　— *John Greisch, CEO, Hill-Rom Holdings, Inc.*

"David zeroes in on the most important activity of leadership—engagement—by communicating context, and he does it by offering a wealth of practical insights leaders can use tomorrow to create clarity and purpose for employees."

　　—*Susan Hunsberger, SVP, Global Business Services, Nielsen*

"A core value of ITW is decentralization… positioning our businesses close to their customers and markets around the globe. This helps us deliver the products and services our customers value and need as efficiently as possible. But it also puts a premium on how we communicate with each other…as individuals and as an organization. **David Grossman's principles and fundamentals for effective communications are constant reminders that to truly make progress, we need to share information across our company in the right way at the right time with the right people. Whether you run a small, family-owned business or a complex, global public enterprise, communications is one of the critical factors that will drive growth and success."**

　　—*David B. Speer, Chairman and CEO, Illinois Tool Works, Inc.*

"Once again, David Grossman proves why he's one of the most sought-after communications experts in the field. From 'The Se7en Deadly Sins of Leadership' to Communicating with Millennials, David offers thoughtful and impactful advice that can help all of us connect more effectively with our stakeholders, and frankly, do our jobs better."

　　— *Jim Sabourin, Vice President, Corporate Communications, Unum Group*

"Like Tom Peters' outstanding works, or McLuhan/Fiore's classic, *The Medium is the Message*, Grossman's entertaining book mixes substance and style, wit and inspiration, pragmatism and possibility. It's a heartening reminder that business writing needn't be boring."

　　—*Frank J. Oswald, Consultant, Frank J. Oswald, LLC*

"You can't not read this book if you're serious about a career in corporate communications. In fact, I believe it should be required reading for all communication majors and managers alike."
— *Susan Heitsch, VP, Communications, Financial Services Industry*

"Practical, wise, smartly designed—an example of what it recommends to its readers."
— *Jon Iwata, Senior Vice President, Marketing and Communications, IBM Corporation*

"Connecting with our staff is now more important than ever. But rapidly evolving employee expectations and job requirements, combined with dynamics of demographics, lifestyle, and culture, makes this very challenging. David's book provides useful advice for planning and executing communication programs that work."
— *Eric Deaton, Executive Vice President – Strategy, HAVI Global Solutions*

"I highly recommend David's second book—*You Can't Not Communicate 2*. **His approach in helping organizations solve business challenges through simple, powerful and effective communications and the process he brings to create those communications is unparalleled. If you aren't using the principles that he teaches, you are not optimizing the power of your people."**
—*Susan Schmitt, Senior Vice President, Human Resources, Rockwell Automation*

"In *You Can't Not Communicate 2*, David does an excellent job of helping leaders understand why effective communication is so critical. **He is very sensitive to the fact that leaders may not know just how powerful their messages are and know how to communicate those messages to a range of employees. This book is a great resource and is designed for leaders to take it in at one sitting or go to for bites of information when needed. As a change management expert, I highly recommend this book not just for leadership, but also change agents in order to make change happen successfully."**
— *Jeanenne LaMarsh, Founder & CEO, LaMarsh & Associates, Inc.*

"I started paging through, and then I was captured. I started turning down corners of pages with GREAT stuff. They're almost all turned down. I read it all. It reads like a conversation with a good (and very WISE) friend."
— *Kathleen L. Lewton, APR, Fellow PRSA, Principal, Lewton, Seekins & Trester*

"Through his work with some of the world's top companies, David Grossman has a great vantage point to see some of the best corporate leaders ... and the worst. He can also see patterns and trends that are often invisible to the rest of us who have limited points of view. **David's got the innate ability to turn his observations into recommendations that can, in turn, transform some of the worst leaders into some of the best. His newest book is a great how-to guide for today's leaders and those who aspire to lead tomorrow."**
—*Brad Whitworth, ABC, IABC Fellow, Senior Communication Manager, Cisco*

YOU CAN'T **NOT** COMMUNICATE 2

More Proven Communication Solutions
that Power the Fortune 100

HOW TOP LEADERS **DIFFERENTIATE THEMSELVES**

by DAVID GROSSMAN, ABC, APR, Fellow PRSA

To Avi, who's rocked my world in ways I never could have imagined.
Being your Dad is pure bliss.

A LEADER'S PERSPECTIVE

What We Learned From 60 Percent Communication

Communication is key. There can be no sustained successes and results without effective communication. We all know this to be true.

But as is often the case, we need to be actively reminded of some basic truths in order to measure not just how true they are, but what it takes to make things happen on a daily basis. Knowing that communication is important is not nearly enough. We need to measure how a lack of effective practice can hinder efforts and lead to dysfunctional organizations.

Over the past three years, I've had the honor of leading a great organization and an iconic brand through major changes. My personal evolution from CFO to CEO of this team, along with our trials and errors, can serve as a reminder to leaders at all levels and in any industry of what happens when communication is only 60 percent effective.

Getting it Right Takes Input

A few years ago, we sold one of our brands, which represented about 30 percent of our total business.

We always try to put our people first, and care a great deal about how we handle such situations. We therefore spent a lot of time preparing internal communications about the sale. This included detailing action plans and creating communication plans around reshaping the organization—down to the last employee hired. Once we went through the process, which went as smoothly as can be expected from an operational perspective, we asked for feedback from our people. We were surprised to learn that—although we got the thumbs up for effective, transparent, timely, and thoughtful communication—we got the thumbs down on…getting input.

> "I, for one, dislike being told to execute something without it being explained properly, and as importantly, ***without being asked for my opinion.***"

Getting it right is not sufficient if people feel that their opinion is not valued, their input not requested. And therefore, we never got it as right as we should have. I learned recently from David Grossman that this is called "two-way communication." The concept simply did not exist in our organization. But it makes sense. I, for one, dislike being told to execute something without it being explained properly, and as importantly, without being asked for my opinion. Only if those two conditions are met can I commit to a plan.

This is self-evident, and yet we missed it repeatedly because the concept was not part of our culture.

A Complex Message Creates Fuzzy Strategy

Our Motel 6 / Studio 6 brand went through a fast-paced business transformation over the past three years. This meant revisiting every single aspect of our business model, leaving no stone unturned.

To achieve this, we had to think broadly about our organization. With our five-year strategic plan in place, we then focused on going deeper, not wider.

Moving from wider to deeper, we took the pulse of the organization through our yearly employee survey. We learned that 50 percent of our General Managers and their teams in the field (i.e., the most critical people in our organization) had at best, a fuzzy idea of what we'd been trying to achieve over the past three years.

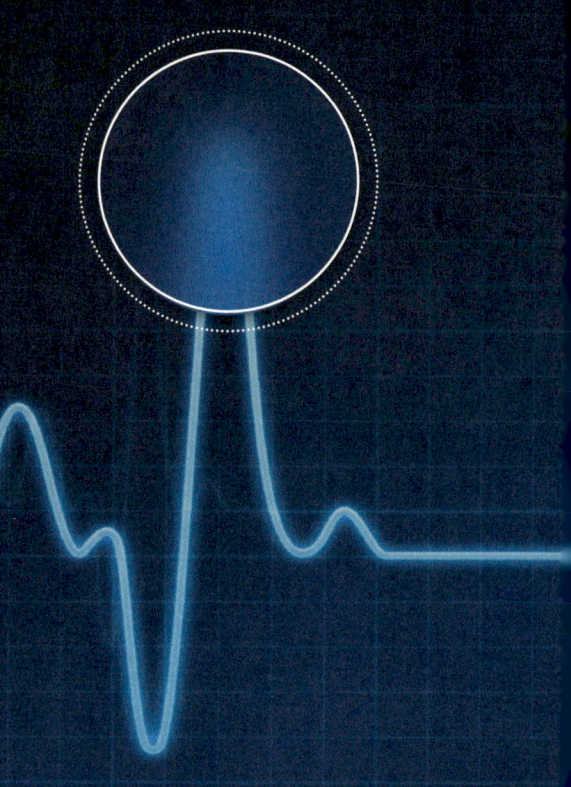

Once again we learned that, although all our goals were met, our "command-and-control" approach left a good deal of our key people less committed than they could have been. This was in spite of a very intensive, comprehensive communication campaign.

Where did we fail?

First, in two-way communication. We didn't ask people to repeat and clarify the information, or give everyone a chance for input.

Second, we failed to communicate a "hierarchy-proof" message. We didn't make the message basic enough, or repeat it often enough in its simplest way so that it could be understood and remembered by all—up to the most recently hired housekeeper—irrespective of the layers of hierarchy passing the message out. As we were preparing our executive team to present our five-year brand strategy to senior management, we wanted to ensure that communication would be a top priority this time around. We asked our senior management to first align around the strategy, and then to help us choose the words to make this relevant to the rest of the organization.

It soon became apparent that, when asked to put this in their own words, most leaders who had aligned behind the exact same strategy hours before, suddenly started to introduce variations of their own. In doing so, they were in fact, demonstrating different aspirational goals, which, in turn, made our strategy fuzzy.

I came to realize that, although we'd been refining our strategy over a two- to three-year period, we never had a clear explanation about all the aspects of that strategy—which we promptly arranged. It then became easier to ask our senior management to align, in their own words, behind the same goals.

It seems so obvious—but how easy it is to think that all angles of the strategy have been communicated when, in fact, only some aspects of it had been communicated beyond top leadership.

"How easy it is to think that all angles of the strategy have been communicated when, in fact, only some aspects of it had been communicated beyond top leadership."

Communication Failures Mean Big Frustration

Our executive team learned this lesson the hard way recently. Having refined the strategy, we aligned all top leaders and worked out the communication for our coming brand project; it was time to take the executive team on a team-building activity.

Two of the exercises were aimed at demonstrating what happens when communication fails. In one exercise, we ended up with two senior executives stranded like pelicans on a pole for the better part of an hour. The second exercise left part of the team so frustrated and disoriented by what seemed like an easily-avoidable communication failure that tempers flared! It literally took 50 minutes to bring the whole team down to Earth.

This failure to communicate was due to everyone in the chain trying to get too much context, as opposed to simply asking the question of their peers: "what do you need me to ask and do?"

This is where David Grossman and his team have been invaluable to Accor and Motel 6 / Studio 6. By having him involved as we were closing a successful, yet stressful, chapter in our history, we were able to learn from our mistakes. By putting communication at the center of our next strategic chapter, we dramatically increased our chance of success. Our next step is all about improving quality and therefore customer perception, and taking advantage of our strong DNA to improve consistency across our 1,100-strong network of Motel 6 / Studio 6 properties.

To get there, we're shooting for a GREAT, consistent delivery. Functional corporate projects were the foundation. Going forward, it's all about ensuring that everyone, down to the last hired housekeeper, understands that by bringing GREAT to work every day, he or she will help us reach our goals and make his or her environment a better place. In other words, their commitment defines our success.

Communication Can Be Taught, and It Takes Work

All those great skills that David is helping build across our organization can be taught. Some leaders get that...some don't; all have to work at communication.

And all of our leaders know that we will be holding each other accountable to a higher level of commitment and communication. Building on the wisdom shared in his last volume, this newest book by David Grossman explains what it takes to communicate effectively to strengthen your organization to 100 percent.

From understanding the potential return on your communication investment, to connecting with the people whose commitment is essential to your success, you'll find practical and useful ideas you can put immediately to work. Some concepts may seem simple; others might seem like common sense. In our experience, knowing communication is important and doing it right are two different things. This book will help you better understand and execute the important communication work—from messages to measurement and steps in between—that will help you consistently deliver on your business goals.

As our operational leaders have been practicing their communication skills, all have found that the key to drive results is to actively engage people. And, to achieve engagement of your employees, you can't not communicate.

Olivier Poirot
CEO, Accor North America and Motel 6 / Studio 6

Contents

I've been gratified and humbled by the response to my first book, *You Can't **NOT** Communicate: Proven Communication Solutions That Power the Fortune 100.* The notion that we communicate with or without intention has struck a chord with many leaders, and driven them to work on one of the most important competencies they need to succeed—the ability to communicate effectively. In this edition, I share more communication solutions that work, with an emphasis on those challenges that might be less common but are no less critical. Once again, the suggestions are proven and I've seen them work—irrespective of the economy, industry, or the leader's style or personality.

In the end, my point-of-view on communication remains the same. Since we communicate whether we want to or not, it's in our best interest to get good at it.

Every day, we make a choice—to communicate in a planful and purposeful way, or to wing it. We choose to help our staffs understand how they fit in and help us drive business results, or allow them to come up with their own priorities and conclusions. We choose to work on this learned skill and continue to develop ourselves, or make excuses about a lack of time, or how communication is a "soft" skill and not essential.

We think most employees across the globe would agree that the majority of the problems in business today lie in the absence of good communication. George Bernard Shaw had it right when he pointed out a common problem: the illusion that communication has taken place. More and more leaders choose to wing their communication, and then spend time cleaning up the mess and re-building strained relationships.

Time and again, we're reminded that effective communication produces results—greater shareholder value, increased revenue and profitability, decreased costs, and improved productivity.

For some leaders, teams, and companies, the result of their collective efforts to improve the communications climate has been remarkable.

For others, the choices made and unwillingness to take a hard look in the mirror have negatively impacted their results and the morale of their organizations. An already-skeptical and confused employee is even more de-motivated when input is not sought, plans are not shared, and critical decisions are not explained. It's no wonder that many employees perceive that "management" doesn't know what they're doing, and there is plenty of material for the reality TV show, "Undercover Boss." I suppose it wouldn't make great TV to follow some of the highly-visible senior leaders with whom we're fortunate enough to work. I can tell you these leaders make great bosses, and most importantly, they make the people around them feel valued.

My hope is that this book will provide additional tips, techniques, and strategies that work for those leaders who want to do better, especially in those less-common-but-still-critical defining moments. Effective communication done well is tough, but well worth the effort. I also hope this book will serve as a wake-up call for those who have yet to begin the journey to communicate with purpose. We all can be more effective communicators, someone might just need to show you how.

David Grossman, ABC, APR, Fellow PRSA

Founder & CEO

The Grossman Group

{ ACKNOWLEDGEMENTS }

First off, I'm grateful to our clients. From those who first believed in me when I left McDonald's Corporation to chase my dream, to those today who put their trust in the methodology we've built over the past decade, it's a privilege to be your **thought**partner™. I never take for granted your partnership. I am truly grateful for the amazing company we keep.

To the brilliant team at The Grossman Group, it's upon your broad shoulders that I stand. You are the get-it-done team, and I'm incredibly proud of our work. In starting the agency, I knew there had to be a better way for companies and consultants to work together. You bring that vision to life beautifully for our clients' defining and every day moments.

I owe a huge debt to my teachers, mentors, students, and family from whom I have learned over the years. You have been open to my barrage of questions and have been patient as I tried to understand how everything works, especially human behavior. Your wisdom and many of your lessons are in this book. I also am grateful to those from whom I continue to learn. I appreciate your openness to my curiosity and wonder about what makes great leaders tick.

I've always been a voracious reader; second only to my constant asking of questions. I'm grateful to my partner, Steve, who asked me a defining-moment question a few years back: "When are you going to stop reading everyone else's books and write one of your own?" From a simple yet powerful question came *You Can't NOT Communicate* and subsequently this book. For all it takes to be married to me, I thank you for your love and support.

The Business of Communicating

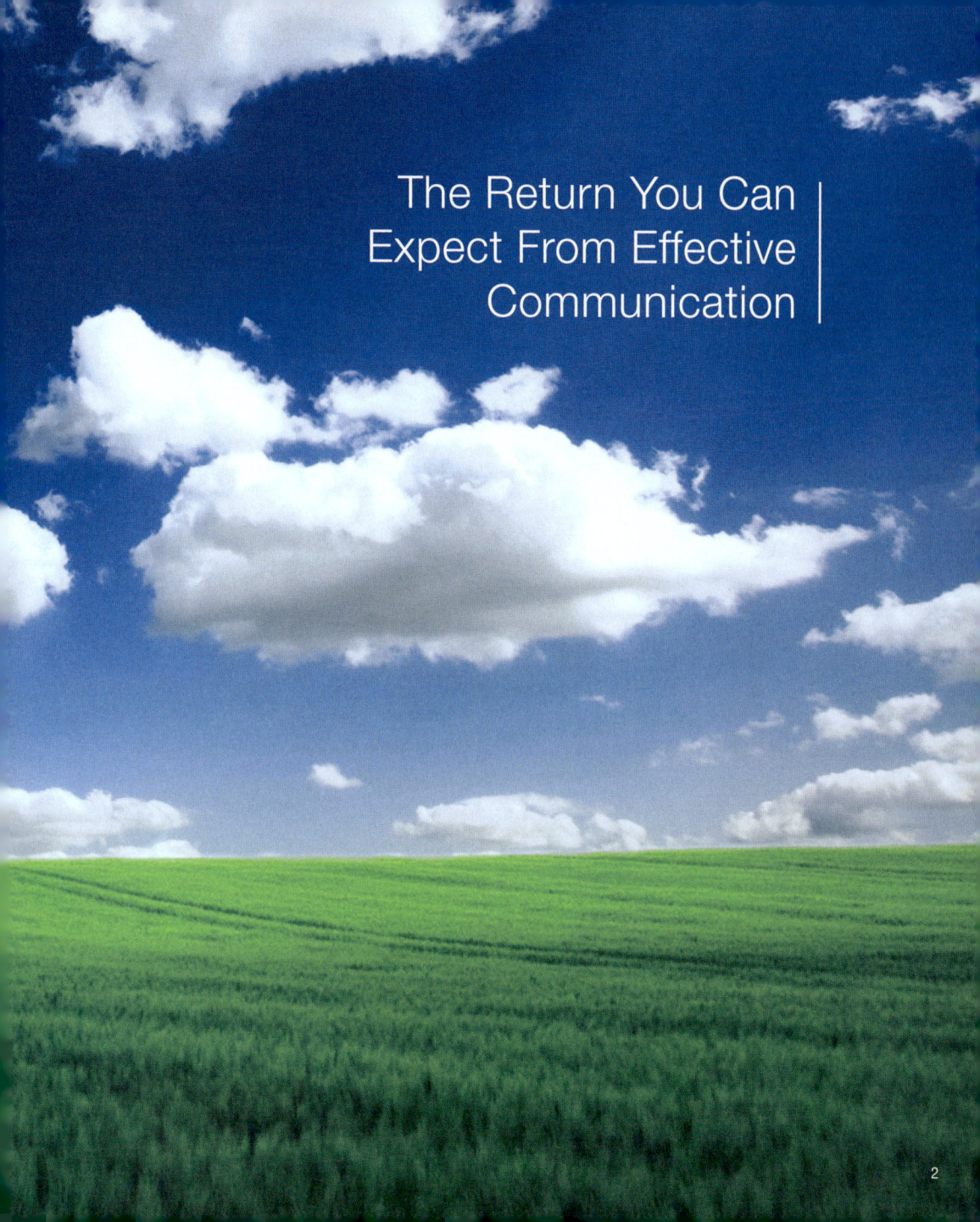

The Return You Can Expect From Effective Communication

Starting thought

The Ultimate "To Do" For Any Leader—Without Question

One of my favorite *Harvard Business Review* articles is entitled, "What Only the CEO Can Do," written by former Procter & Gamble CEO A. G. Lafley[1], turnaround expert extraordinaire. In his thought-provoking article, he reflects on discussions he had with Peter Drucker, other CEOs, and management gurus a few years back about a central question: What are CEOs uniquely qualified to do (you also can glean the role of leaders in general from their conclusions)?

First off, I love the question, and I think each of us should ask ourselves what only we can do for our organization because that helps us focus on the most highly-valued and valuable tasks.

Here's where they netted out for CEOs:

1. **Defining and interpreting the meaningful "outside"**
2. **Regularly answering the two-part question: What business are we in and what business are we not in?**
3. **Balancing sufficient yield in the present with necessary investment in the future**
4. **Shaping the values and standards of the organization**

The critical core competency in three out of four of these is communication.

Once again, we have some powerful ammunition on the essential role, and often-misunderstood superpower, we call communications. Like it or not, leaders are accountable not only for operating their organizations, but for shaping the vision and inspiring their employees to thrive. Communication is at the center of it all.

What are you uniquely qualified to contribute?

"The two words *'information'* and *'communication'* are often used interchangeably, but they signify quite different things. Information is giving out; communication is getting through."

– Sydney J. Harris, Journalist

Communication as the CEO's Bottom Line

In looking at the conclusions of A.G. Lafley's CEO discussion group, here are the connections I see:

Defining and interpreting the meaningful "outside."

This is about aligning everyone to a common context for the organization. Each of us comes into the workplace with our own context because of how we were raised, our experience, background, etc. That's a wonderful thing because we need diversity more than ever today, especially when innovation is essential for success. However, to make smart business plans and decisions, employees need to understand the collective context we all agree on as an organization. This may or may not be in sync with how a specific individual thinks about our customers, the marketplace, or the top strengths we need to leverage as an organization.

REFLECTION POINT: How do you define the "outside" for your team and set the context for them (as well as help them make their job relevant in that context)?

Regularly answering the two-part question: What business are we in and what business are we not in?

This is about which of our core competencies we will leverage as an organization. We might be able to succeed in a number of ways, but where will we focus (note the emphasis on what will not get done)? Where are the boundaries for what we do? This two-part question also further helps set the context. A number of years ago, McDonald's began to diversify by adding a number of other food-related businesses before it got back to basics and realized its core competency is being in the hamburger business, not in pizza or Mexican food.

REFLECTION POINT: How do you provide focus around what your team does and doesn't do without stifling thinking and innovation?

Balancing sufficient yield in the present with necessary investment in the future.

You can't win them all.

Shaping the values and standards of the organization.

This is about determining the core DNA for the organization—who we are and what we stand for—especially when times get tough or crises hit. Unfortunately, many times this effort is only paid lip service and turns into wordsmithing among the senior management team. Worse yet, the communications team is creating the values instead of facilitating the process of alignment. To effectively shape the organization's values and standards, leadership must be aligned around not only the concepts, but the behaviors and daily actions that are required, including the critical role leaders play in building an aligned culture. The systems in the organization, such as performance management, also need to be synced up so words and actions follow. It's a truism that what gets measured is what gets focused on and done.

REFLECTION POINT: How do you continually connect the dots between your work and your organization's values?

The Business Case for the leader**communicator**™
Today's business environment is one of uncertainty and change.

Many factors in our changing environment force businesses and leaders to behave differently:

- Employees expect **more** of their employers, as businesses demand more quality and productivity from them.
- Customer service is becoming the consummate differentiator.
- You have to connect the dots for people if you want them to understand and act on your business strategy, increase productivity or improve customer service.
- The best business plan is worthless if people don't know where their company is going or what to do to help it get there.
- Nearly 50 percent of employees say they don't understand their company's business strategies or what is required for success[2].

In the end, everything you need to get done is through people:

- The role of leadership communications no longer applies solely to a few C-level executives…or to supervisors.
- Today, we need everyone inside our organizations to lead—no matter where they sit, or whether they have direct reports or not. Even traditional managers must lead.
- A leader's ability to engage and connect each employee to the organization is key to achieving performance and long-term goals.

We've entered the dawn of the leader**communicator**, where you can't separate communication from leadership.

To connect the dots, we must engage people in the business strategy and help them understand how they fit in. Then, manage messages so we influence the decision moments and the discretionary effort people choose to give (or not give).

leader**communicator** *(lédr • komûni-kàtor)* **n.**

1. understands communication begins and ends with himself or herself **2.** understands that communication is an instrument of strategy, and a strategy in itself **3.** understands employees' strategic communication needs **4.** plans communication; is aware communication doesn't just "happen" **5.** ensures actions follow words; knows people search for meaning in actions **6.** recognizes that most problems in business today lie in the absence of real communication, and facilitates dialogue to create shared meaning

TIP:
The C-Factor: Communication factors for top leaders

To drive effective communication, leaders must:

- Be visible
- Communicate frequently
- Be honest, open, trustworthy, and candid
- Understand that everything they say and do communicates something (including what they don't say or do)
- Answer questions employees have (ideally before they ask them)
- Be engaged in developing/planning communication (so they're energetic and passionate about what they say)
- Ask employees for their input and use it
- Engage the Communications function as a business partner

Critical Factors Impacting Communication Today

Consider the following factors that are constantly changing, creating ever-shifting contexts and engendering employee insecurity, uncertainty, and fear:

Change #1
Business Environment

Talk is cheap in corporate America—especially when it comes to leaders and their ability to build and maintain trust. These days, organizations are under attack and protecting every asset; the pressure is mounting for leaders to find the answers. Employees, who need to stay focused and productive now more than ever, are numb from fear of losing their jobs, of taking on more work, of the unknown, or of a combination of all three.

Trust between employees and their employers is at an all-time low, while skepticism and concern is high. A 2010 Maritz Research poll[3] found:

- Only 11 percent of employees strongly agree that their managers show consistency between their words and their actions.

- Only seven percent strongly agree that they trust senior leaders to look out for their best interest.

- Approximately one fifth of respondents disagree that their company's leader is completely honest and ethical.

- One quarter of respondents disagree that they trust management to make the right decisions in times of uncertainty.

Those are high numbers!

And get this: Nearly two-thirds (63 percent) of respondents with strong trust in management would be happy to spend the rest of their career with their present company. This compares to only seven percent of respondents who have weak trust in management.

Today, employees are putting leaders of all levels on notice that when it comes to earning trust, they need to work harder. Economic meltdowns and corporate scandals have led to greater expectations and regulations around transparency, and remain front-and-center in employees' minds. The playing field has changed.

Change #2
Employee-Employer Contract

The relationship between employers and employees is changing every day. Businesses are demanding more quality and productivity as they face intense pressures to satisfy Wall Street and shareholders. At the same time, employees know there is no such thing as job security.

In the wake of significant economic and business challenges and foreign competition, companies in many industries are making cuts across all areas of their operations—including employee benefits, training, and development. Meanwhile, other organizations are dealing with increased pressure from outsourcing to overseas call centers and manufacturing.

Either way, it's becoming increasingly difficult for employees to expend discretionary effort and to stay committed when the very foundation of what they expect from their employer can change in an instant.

In light of this diminishing loyalty, one has to wonder, does the employee-employer contract as we've known it still exist? The answer is no. The old "contract" has been replaced by what I call the new "deal," which many organizations are working on redefining today. Those that aren't are seeing even greater disillusionment and mistrust because expectations are not in sync between employee and employer.

The new deal is more of an understanding than a contract, yet it can still be stated explicitly. Organizations must make it crystal clear what they expect from their employees, and what employees can expect from the organization.

Change #3
Technology

The Internet is the great leveler when it comes to accessing information. Not only is it easier for employees to get information more quickly, but with the proliferation of vehicles like blogs, it's also a lot easier for them to make information available to others. At the same time, organizations are sometimes challenged with getting news to employees before the media and bloggers shape perception and share news of key issues—like stock prices or the abilities of leadership.

Social media has taken hold in myriad ways that can make employees feel more connected and more informed, but that can also create a false sense of interaction and relationship-building.

Organizations need to find new and different ways to get—and hold—employees' attention and engagement, and they need to get to them first and in meaningful ways.

"For having lived long, I have experienced many instances of being obliged—by better information or fuller consideration—to change opinions, even on important subjects, which I once thought right but found to be otherwise."

– Benjamin Franklin

Change #4
The Economy and Global Events

As the world becomes smaller and global competition intensifies, organizations are focused on new and different ways to boost performance and productivity.

Blurred geographic boundaries, combined with the force of global events, economic crises in various parts of the world, and intense economic pressures, require organizations to make tough decisions that impact employees at all levels. This directly influences communication as organizations try to find the best way to communicate with employees in different countries, who speak multiple languages, who have varying immediate concerns, and who operate within a variety of cultures and norms. Organizations still need to communicate their messages, but in a way that is faster and appeals to the various cultural nuances, all the while contending with increased scrutiny from the public and government oversight.

Today's Communication Environment is Drastically Different

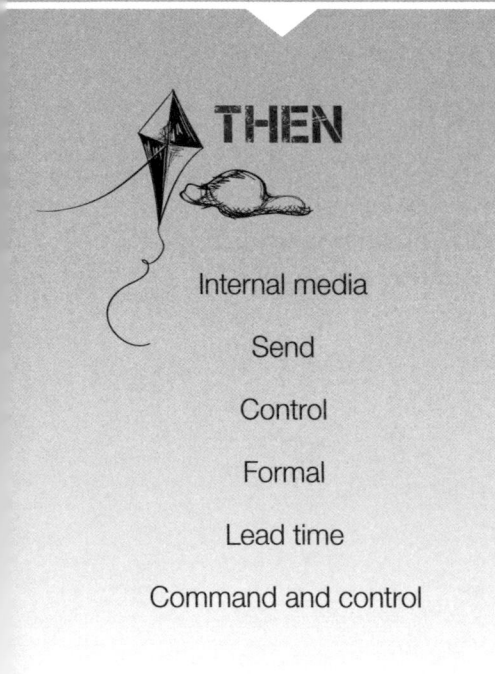

THEN

Internal media

Send

Control

Formal

Lead time

Command and control

NOW

Face-to-face, social media

Engage, participate, involve

Be part of the conversation

Informal

Everything instant

Influence and persuade

Compelling Research on the Value of the Employee Advocate

A study commissioned by IBM in seven countries[4] including Brazil, Germany, Spain, Italy, India, Singapore, and Japan, asked respondents to share opinions of several major brands. One of the questions asked respondents to rank what has the biggest influence on their opinion of the companies they were asked about in the survey.

What were deemed most and least influential was consistent across the seven countries. Least influential were news stories, direct marketing, and advertising. Most influential—#1 in five of the seven countries and #2 in the other two—was "personal experiences with employees of that company."

A subsequent study probed deeper on what was meant by "employee." Respondents did not just mean a company's sales person or customer-facing employee, but anyone who works—or worked—for that company. And for "personal experience," respondents didn't just mean face-to-face. They included online interactions, such as reading an individual's blog or being part of their social network.

Good Employee Communication Can Improve an Organization and Drive Business Success by Turning Strategy Into Action

Good internal communication gets the message out, but great internal communication helps employees connect the dots between the overarching business strategy and their individual roles. When it's good, it informs; when it's great, it engages employees and moves them to action. Quite simply, it helps people and organizations be even better.

The reality is, despite all the new and timely communication channels, despite the flurries of emails that define today's workplace, despite meetings and memos and more, research shows that the majority of companies aren't getting through to employees to help them connect the dots:

- **Only 37 percent** of employees have a clear understanding of what their organization is trying to do and why.
- **1 in 5** employees are enthusiastic about their organization's and team's goals.
- **20 percent** have a clear "line of sight" between their tasks and the organization's or team's goals[5].

Those are alarmingly low numbers when you consider that a disconnect between employees and the business significantly detracts from organizational success, profit, and growth.

Consider these findings[6]:

- Effective employee communication is a leading indicator of financial performance and a driver of employee engagement.
- Companies that have highly effective communicators had 47 percent higher total returns to shareholders over five years (2004 – 2009) compared to companies with less effective communication.
- Only 14 percent of survey participants are explaining the terms of the Employee Value Proposition (EVP)—what employees can expect from the company—to their employees.
- While only three in 10 organizations are training managers to deal openly with resistance to change, highly effective communicators are more than three times as likely to help leaders and managers communicate better as the least effective communicators.
- Companies that have less-effective communicators are three times as likely as highly effective communicators to report having no formal communication measurement.

Communication is more than a "feel good" part of any organization. It separates mediocre companies from great ones, lousy leaders from those who are truly outstanding, and discontented employees from those who are engaged and excited about work.

Study Links Communication with Improved Patient Outcomes

A recent study released in *The Annals of Medicine*[7] showed that communication and culture impact patient outcomes more than any other factor…even the best equipment or surgeons.

The researchers focused on hospitals with the lowest and highest mortality rates from heart attacks, and compared their performance with themes from more than 150 interviews with physicians, nurses, and administrators.

According to the study, what really mattered was simply this: **a cohesive organizational vision that focused on communication and support of all efforts to improve care.** *"It's how people communicate, the level of support, and the organizational culture that trump any single intervention or any single strategy that hospitals frequently adopt,"* said Elizabeth H. Bradley, senior author and faculty director of the Yale Global Health Leadership Institute at Yale University, as quoted in the *New York Times*[8].

Earlier studies suggested other explanations for the difference in outcomes such as income, affiliation with an academic medical center, and number of beds, among others.

"A lot of people think that you have to go to a really big city teaching hospital with really expensive equipment," Dr. Bradley said. *"But we didn't find that to be true."*

"We have to focus on the relationships inside the hospital and be committed to making the organization work. It isn't expensive and it isn't rocket science, but it requires a real commitment from everyone."

Go Figure! What Would Your Investment Be Worth?

If you had invested $100 in 2004 in the companies from the Towers Watson Communication ROI Study[9] that have highly effective communication, what would your investment have been worth in 2009?

a) $100   **c)** $120

b) $116   **d)** $130

The answer: d) $130

Not a bad return in comparison to the least effective companies (worth $83) or the moderately effective companies (worth $100).

TIP:

Did you know?

Disengaged employees have a staggering effect on business. Recent studies[10] have shown that lower productivity has an estimated economic impact of $300 billion per year, while increased workplace injury, illness, turnover, absence, and fraud have an economic impact estimated at $1 trillion per year. This is felt around the world at a global level, but it also has very personal and immediate effects on organizations, departments, teams and, as a result, individual employees.

The Net, Net of Effective Communication

In the end, what's the payoff to communicating well?

Employees understand the big picture and how they fit in.

They feel valued, listened to, and like an important part of the team and the organization.

Employees are more productive when there is meaning to their work.

As a result, they contribute more and feel better about their contribution—as well as the organization—so they stay on the job and help move the business forward.

Better leaders.

Communication isn't just tactical anymore; it's about strategy. In this context, leaders are better able to understand employee needs and how to meet those needs to motivate, inspire, and engage them.

Vigilant managers who have an ear to the ground.

For managers and organizations to attract, create, and retain an engaged workforce, they must be committed for the long haul. Building the trust and credibility to keep employees engaged requires effort, but it's worth it. It takes only seconds to lose employee connection and interest.

A culture of communication.

The employee engagement journey is a continuous one. Communication is not an "event." It is a continuing process. You must work every day to ask the right questions, answer others appropriately, and communicate openly and honestly with employees. When they see you making that extra effort, they'll do the same. By moving away from lip service and toward positive action, you drive positive business results.

Organizations that understand, prioritize, and constantly strive to achieve better internal communication are a breed apart. They achieve trust and credibility. They enable employees to do their jobs better. They create a constructive workplace that encourages growth and a common sense of purpose.

From all this, there can only be one result: higher levels of performance and better business results.

What Employees Want

Meeting Their Needs
Drives Engagement

"The most basic of all human needs is the need to understand and be understood. The best way to understand people is to listen to them."

– Ralph Nichols, Author

Starting thought

What Every Employee Wants

I read an article in *USA Today* about how many consumers are "app-y" because they can use their mobile devices to store their gift wish lists. That got me thinking: If employees in today's global organizations were to develop their collective "wish list," what would be on it?

- **Less BS and more humanity**—Enough beating-around-the-bush or, worse yet, "spinning" of messages. Employees want to know what's happening and why in a direct way. Tell me what you know when you know it. Chances are, you're waiting too long after getting key information to communicate it.

- **Understanding of your expectations**—People rise to the expectations set for them. Many problems in business are caused by a lack of understanding of expectations or a misunderstanding of what's needed and expected.

- **More listening (to me)**—Stop talking so much. Ask for input and feedback. I am more likely to support what I help create. Stop the monologues and talking at me; let's have real, two-way conversations.

- **Take action on employee suggestions**—The action might be to loop back with the employee to share appreciation for their thoughts, and help them understand why you're not implementing their suggestion for an alternate approach. The action is closing the feedback loop, which can be as worthwhile as implementing an employee's suggestion.

- **Show me you care (in a genuine way)**—Find out what's important to me, and please be sure to acknowledge critical milestones that are important to me.

- **Empathize with me**—Pause and imagine how I'm feeling. Show you hear me, and validate my feelings. The payoff is an employee who knows you care; at the same time, you gather information that's useful to motivating that employee.

- **Recognize and appreciate me**—Say "thank you" for a job well done. Reinforce very specifically the behaviors you want to continue to see. At a two-way communication training recently, a woman asked whether she needed to reward and recognize someone on her team for "just doing his job." Absolutely. Jobs don't inspire and motivate people; leaders do.

So that's my short list. Best of all, these "gifts" on the wish list are free. No coupons required. You don't need to fight the crowds. All that's needed might be a little training or coaching to help you improve your leadership impact. And that could be the best gift you give yourself (and your staff).

Which of these skills would have the greatest impact on your results?

I Am Your Employee

Employees come to work for different reasons, have different goals, and are motivated by different things. How well do you know your employees? (If you know them well, chances are you would hear them saying something like this.)

I am your employee...

I've been told I am part of the human capital equation and very important here. So, if I may, I have a couple of thoughts I'd like to share.

It's about why I chose this organization...and what I expect from my employment experience. I need to feel valued, to be treated with respect and to know my supervisor cares about me. I need regular information from my manager, but still need to hear from senior leaders on broader company issues.

I need to know how I will benefit when I produce good results. And I need regular, tangible, specific, constructive feedback about my work.

So you see, if I am really a part of your human capital, I need to feel like the 'human' aspect is important to you, not like I am a commodity.

When I can do good work and get back from you what I need, I couldn't be happier. I wake up in the morning eager to do a good job. During those times I feel fulfilled and happy with my work life. I'm ready to go 'above and beyond' when you need me to. But, if you ask more and more from me without acknowledging what I am contributing, telling me I have value or telling me how I'm doing, that makes me frustrated and leaves me unfulfilled. I start to question whether coming here was the right thing to do.

If you don't meet my expectations, how can you expect me to meet yours, especially if you don't make your expectations clear?

And if I have expectations that I don't share with you, as my employer, how can you know what motivates, energizes, and supports me?

It's pretty much about communication; between us; between my supervisor and me; and between my fellow employees and me.

And good communication is tough. I am bombarded by messages and communications clutter, and appreciate having a choice of media. I am willing to take the initiative to find out some of the information I need. But I may not realize the responsibility I have to seek out information. And I'm not sure you realize how much I need to feel included in the process.

I will be more engaged if I have had a chance to provide input up front, especially in decisions that affect my job. My behavior is a consequence of how I'm treated and rewarded.

When you get my attention, I am listening to what you say…more importantly I am watching what you do!…*I am your employee!*

The Questions Employees Have (and You Need To Answer)

Whether employees ask them or not, the reality is there are several key questions that are on their minds—The Eight Key Questions™.

These questions are a lot like Maslow's hierarchy of needs—which states that only after a person has fulfilled certain levels of needs can he or she begin to move to more complex levels of thought, self-awareness, and understanding of others. In other words, employees' basic needs have to be addressed first before they can begin to think beyond themselves. Employees' core questions are "me"-focused questions that help them understand what's happening around them and what it means to them specifically.

Once the me-focused questions are answered, then employees are able to look beyond themselves. "What's going on?" they often ask as they then become aware of changes or initiatives happening outside their department or function. It's only then that they become interested in the "we"-focused questions, which are focused on the larger organization. The ultimate payoff is when employees ask, "How can I help?" This is an expression of engagement—a willingness to do more—which also demonstrates a strong emotional connection to the organization.

It's important to remember that these are questions that employees think about, and perhaps ask, every day—whether they are new to the organization or veterans. When change happens, as it often does in today's fast-paced business world, employees immediately go back to the me-focused questions. Our job as leaders is to get them back to question eight as quickly as possible. If we don't, that's when business often gets stopped, slowed, or interrupted as employees work through—or are challenged by—change.

8. How can I help?
7. What's our vision and values?
6. How are we doing?
5. What's our business strategy?

we

4. What's going on? — **transition**

3. Does anyone care about me?
2. How am I doing?
1. What's my job?

me

To Engage Employees, Tap Rational and Emotional Factors

To understand how to connect with employees, it is important to recognize that engagement involves both emotional and rational factors relating to work and the overall work experience.

The emotional factors are those that relate to an individual's personal satisfaction and the sense of inspiration and affirmation they get from their work, and from being part of an organization. The rational factors, by contrast, relate to the relationship between the individual and the broader company. An example of this would be an employee's understanding of their role and their team's role, as they relate to the overall company objectives.

You may not realize it, but you're actually engaging employees every time you:

- Help them understand the realities of your business
- Connect the dots between the big picture of your business and what it means to them and their job
- Reinforce that they can trust you
- Ask for their thoughts and feedback
- Ask how they are doing

TIP:

Make the information vacuum work for you

Waiting to communicate until you have all the answers is a risky proposition. Employees just want to know what you know—your "take" —and what you don't know, as well as when you'll have the rest of the information (because they understand when you don't have all the facts or details).

Chances are you know a number of key facts that would be helpful for employees to know (and will stop them from filling the information vacuum themselves with misinformation).

If engagement merely facilitated a more efficient working environment or a friendlier atmosphere, the business imperative to make it a priority wouldn't be as compelling. But when the payoff is employees' extra effort, the willingness to act as a champion, and to advocate for your organization, the desire to provide value every minute of the day, engaging employees is a critical success factor for any organization.

Without Context, There's No Meaning

Every employee comes into the workplace with his or her own context. It's a mix of our upbringing, culture, religion, memories, and experiences, along with other cues and clues from the individual communicating the message. Context influences how we interpret information. It's the glasses through which we look at and understand the world. For example, without context, our business plan is simply words on a page with little if any meaning.

Part of the role we have as leaders is to create a shared vision. That requires a common understanding of context from those who will help us achieve our goals. For example, how do we view the current business situation we're in, and why does the plan just developed make sense? Setting context might involve talking about our current results and management expectations, new customer requirements, and recently acquired competitive data…all of which help us understand the current situation for the business plan, for example, the "why" behind the plan.

So if you want to get from blank stare to "ah-ha," connect the dots between what you say and what the listener already knows. Set the context in terms of where the listener is coming from.

How will you know if you've succeeded? Just ask for playback: "Tell me what you just heard, and give me your reaction to it." In the end, it's the listener who's the final arbiter as to whether he or she "gets it" or not.

TIP:

Employee to manager: don'ts that disengage

Here's what employees say managers don't do. They:

- Don't keep employees informed
- Don't explain the "why" behind decisions
- Don't communicate frequently enough and in a timely way
- Don't update employees on changes happening in the business
- Don't share regular business updates and how the team is performing
- Don't ask for feedback
- Don't ask for or listen to concerns
- Don't act on feedback (or at least close the loop as to why feedback wasn't incorporated into a decision)

Defining That All-important Context: I Like the Sound of That!

One of the core responsibilities of a leader in helping their employees with line-of-sight and sound decision-making is to set the proper context (the other is to make information relevant). As you think about how to set context, below are some of the categories of information to consider.

Ask yourself...to understand what's happening and why, does your team need information on:

- Background/history
- Assumptions
- Strategy
- Reasons behind decisions
- Metrics/success
- Objectives

- Roles
- Milestone checkpoints
- Relative priority
- Knowledge of the stakes
- Decision-making expectations

Go slow to go fast. Providing the right insights and making them relevant to your outcome up front will help your staff make sound decisions and avoid false-starts and re-work. When mistakes happen, ask yourself, "What context did I fail to set?"

TIP:

Survey says...

Recent research we've done with our clients across industries tell us this:

- Employees are confused about where organizations are going and their role in getting there
- They want to hear from their senior leaders more
- They have big questions they need answered about overall strategy and how they fit in
- And, they're looking for meaning...not just answers or words

Tough Decisions Are Easier With Input

Leaders have difficult decisions to make about how to deliver on aggressive goals: grow their business, get ahead of the competition, and control spending, among many others. But they don't have to make the tough calls in a vacuum.

What if they involved employees in the decision-making? It would make their jobs easier, decrease stress, and perhaps—most importantly—it would send a message to employees that they have as great a stake in the business as their leaders do. Involving employees in business decisions can do great things for an organization. It can boost morale and productivity, increase employee satisfaction, and even lead to greater customer satisfaction and cost reductions.

Plus, when employees are involved in solving a business challenge, they're more likely to accept the solution—whatever it may be—because they will have had ownership in reaching the conclusion. The next time you have a decision to make, ask your employees for their input. Present them with the challenge and ask what they would do if they were in your shoes. Not only will it give you insight into where they're coming from, it also will help you build credibility and increase their ownership in what you want to accomplish.

Every time you communicate is an opportunity to find out if your audience "gets" what you're saying. Ask them questions to check for understanding.

You want to know if your audience...	Ask them...
Heard your key messages or if you need more context or detail	*What are your key takeaways from the information I just shared?*
Understands the "why" and "what" behind a change initiative	*What challenges and opportunities do you see with what I've just explained?*
Is comfortable with the messages you're communicating or if they have feedback	*What's your reaction to what I've just shared with you?*
Has any other questions	*What other questions do you have?*

"Everyone's in-box and out-box are full, but I'm concerned we're avoiding the too-hard box."

– Employee, "Fierce Conversations"

TRY IT TODAY

Think about how you are meeting your employees' needs and what you could do to help them be more engaged.

- **Do your employees understand the business goals?** Identify three ways you can share information on the company objectives, strategies, and roles, then check for understanding by asking them to restate what they heard or to share thoughts such as, "What challenges and opportunities do you see with what I've just explained?"

- **Are you focused on what employees need?** Every time you are in front of employees, make a point of talking about how their work relates to the company's success and ask for questions and input.

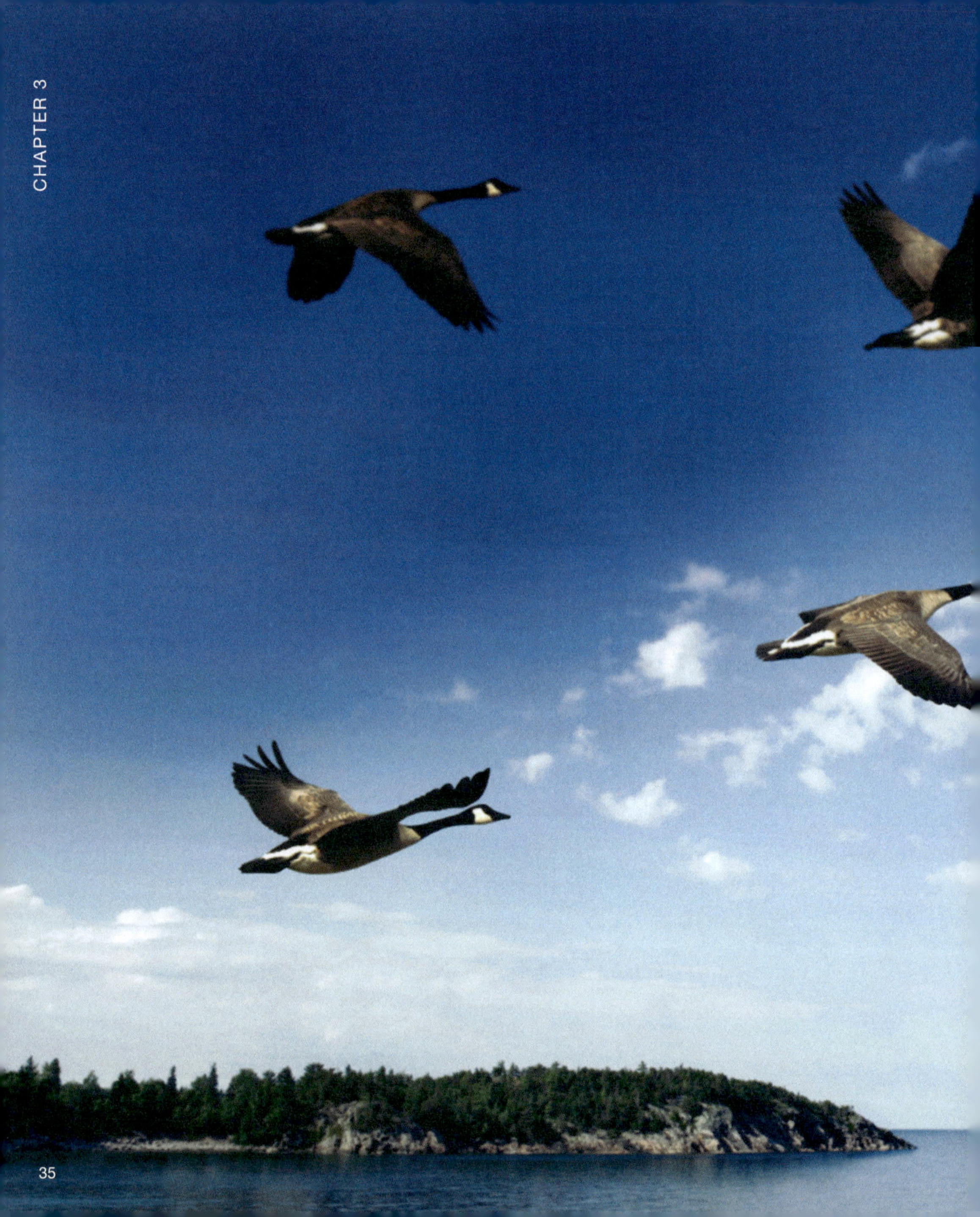

The Leader Differential

Five Steps to Thrive

36

"For a tree to become tall it must
grow tough roots among the rocks."

– Friedrich Nietzsche, Philosopher

Starting thought

Times Have Been Tough For Business

Economic crisis, cutbacks, layoffs, and reduced budgets defined workplace decisions and dynamics. As a result, leaders and decision makers more often found themselves doing responsive triage rather than initiating productive engagement, employee satisfaction, and business evolution.

Whether you're a senior leader, working at an agency counseling clients, or responsible for communications inside a company, you're beginning to understand that there's a "new normal." Setting aside the usual array of workplace challenges—increased globalization, competition in the marketplace, changing workforce demographics, an increase in virtual employees, and further pressures on work/family balance, to name a few—you now face a workforce that is more skeptical and, in some cases, more wounded than ever before.

Sure, thinking about the big effects of something as (seemingly) small as a drop in engagement probably makes you want to pull the covers over your head and go back to bed 'til it's all over.

This is probably even more true if your current communication plan involves staying in survival mode, rather than overhauling your entire strategy to compensate for lost morale. But the truth is, the challenges of the past offer opportunities for the future. With fresh assessment, clear goals, and a path to effective communication—along with empathy, courage, and compassion—you can set your company or clients on the path to not just survive, but thrive in the coming months and years.

How are you making a difference?

1 2 3 4 5

Get a mirror
(for yourself or for your leadership team)

You're Aware That Employees Listen to What You Say, and Also Are Paying Close Attention to What You Do

The truth is that body language speaks, and often louder than words. And there's no better way to think about how others see you than to visualize a mirror that is in front of you all the time.

Reflect on what others are seeing and reading every time they interact with you, and develop the awareness not only to act the role of the leader you want to be, but to role model the actions and characteristics that you would like to see in others.

Great leaders know themselves and have an understanding of how others see them. As a leader, think about putting an actual mirror on your desk as a constant reminder to reflect on your role and on the influence you can have. You need to understand your leadership style and to know that communication and effective management begin and end with you. The more you reflect on your role as a leader, the more that mirror will reflect the positive and influential image that those in the company see too.

"It is one of the commonest of mistakes to consider that the limit of our power of perception is also the limit of all there is to perceive."

– C. W. Leadbeater, Author

TIP:

Role modeling 101

- **Do you want to send a message that you're open and available to your team?** Walk the floors or halls of your company, keep your office door open, or join your team members for lunch or during a break.

- **Want your team to know you're listening?** Repeat or paraphrase what they tell you so they know you not only heard them but are processing/thinking about what they've said.

- **Want your team to know you care about them?** Ask them how they're doing or what's on their mind. And if they offer an idea on something that could be improved, take action on it.

- **Want employees to follow certain procedures?** Use the same procedures yourself, and explain why you're using them and how they help.

1 **2** 3 4 5 | Plan your communication

As With Every Other Strategic Discipline Inside Organizations Today, Communication is Planned From the Beginning With a Clear Assessment of the Business Outcome You Want to Achieve With Each Initiative

If you're a natural communicator, you might be wondering why communicating with your department needs a formal, structured strategy. There are myriad reasons, but the most important one is that "just do it" just doesn't work.

I can tell you from experience that leaders often feel their communication efforts are better spent on external initiatives—initiatives that have the potential to directly affect their bottom line and business growth. But when they begin to add up the collateral damage resulting from a high decline in engagement, they begin to realize the very direct importance of an internal communication strategy.

Like any communication plan, you have to think outcome, audience, message, method, and evaluation. But don't feel like you have to have *all* the information before you communicate.

Waiting to communicate often is paralyzing and inefficient, and it's a sure-fire way to feed the rumor grapevine, potentially sabotaging your initiative before it even gets off the ground. Chances are you already have enough information that is valuable to employees.

How Much Information is Enough Information?

Naturally, it depends on the situation, but in the case, for example, that you've got a big elephant in the room— a reorganization, a high-level executive change, a merger or acquisition, a round of layoffs, or anything else that could be seen by employees as directly threatening their positions at your company— tell them what you know, what you don't know, when you're going to find out additional information, and stamp out myths or misperceptions.

The key here is transparency, which means addressing the issue at hand before it spirals out of control.

A truly good plan creates a well-informed workforce, and a well-informed workforce can be one of the most powerful weapons in your company arsenal.

Difficult messages made easy

It's never easy to communicate difficult information to employees, but with these six essential steps, you can prepare for the toughest conversations:

1. Identify the problem. Are business results not where they should be? Do staffing changes need to be made? Are there undesired behaviors that need to change?

2. Identify your desired outcome. What business result(s) do you seek?

3. Identify your audience. Do you need to inform your entire staff? Is it a small group of employees? Is it one employee? And should they all hear the message at the same time, or should some people hear it first? What do you want your audience(s) to think, feel, and/or do?

4. Structure your key messages/conversation. What will you say (in a calm, constructive way) to employee(s) so that they understand the situation and your concerns?

- Consider how to start the conversation.

- Identify the questions you will ask (to seek input/check for understanding). For example, "Tell me how you feel about what I just said."

- Have stories or examples to share to illustrate your main point.

- Outline specific actions being taken and/or that your employees need to take.

5. Consider how you will say your message. Select the right time and place to have a conversation with privacy and without distraction. Encourage dialogue so you can get real-time insight on how employees are receiving the information, what's on their minds, and if they understand what you are saying.

6. Follow up. Do your employees have questions? What's on their minds? Are you on the path to achieving your business outcome?

1 2 **3** 4 5

Listen first. Listen second.
THEN communicate

There's a Reason We Have Two Ears and One Mouth

Ask the necessary questions first, then actively listen. Then listen some more.

Check your understanding by paraphrasing what you hear and allowing employees to correct you. Let employees vent. Empathize and re-frame issues where needed. Your goal should be to help them understand what's happening, why it's happening, and how it affects them. Get out of your own way, let go of your ego, and understand that it's not about you—and even when it is, your team is more concerned with your leadership style than your personal flaws.

TIP:

Choosing your best communication channel

Once you know what you want to communicate, it's important to think about how you communicate it. Here are some simple tips to keep in mind when choosing a channel to communicate your message most effectively:

Use face-to-face communication when you want to:

- Address topics that require immediate action
- Discuss complex, confidential, or sensitive topics or issues
- Gather immediate feedback and input

Use email when you want to:

- Provide directional, important, and timely information to targeted audiences
- Direct the receiver to a website or online source for more information
- Share detailed information and data

Use voicemail when you want to:

- Communicate urgent, brief messages that require quick action but don't require proof that the communication was made
- Request a same-day or next-day response
- Communicate with team members who are traveling

1 2 3 **4** 5

You're always communicating,
so control the message

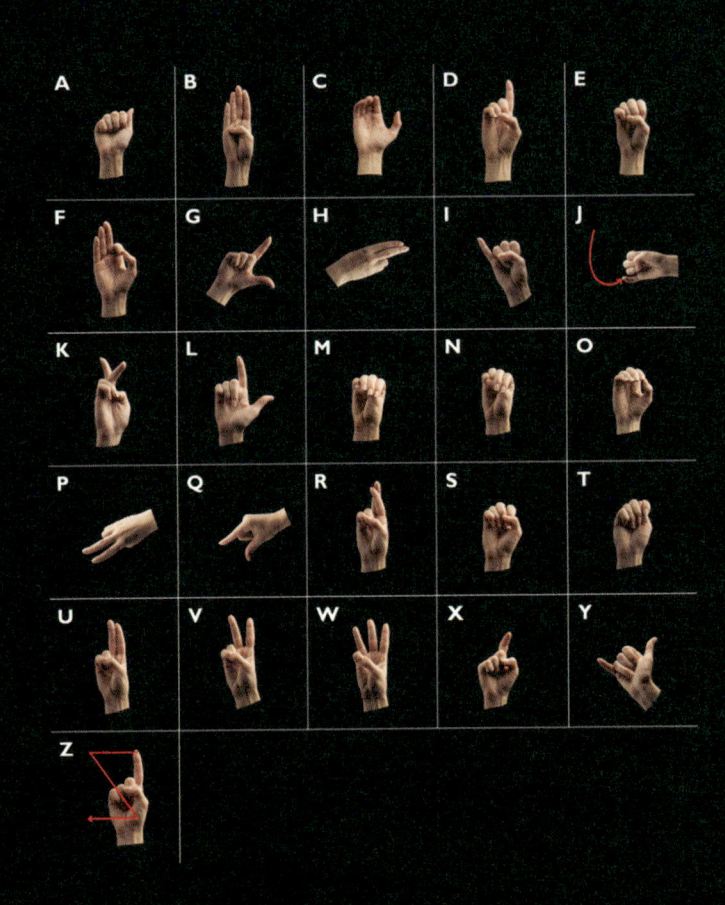

Leaders Are Always Communicating Whether They Intend To or Not
Don't assume that because you're not saying anything, you're
not sending any messages. Your employees will read into your
behavior when you withhold information or avoid communicating
just as much as when you directly and openly communicate. You
may think you're doing your employees a favor by keeping them
out of concerns or by waiting to tell them about change until it's a
foregone conclusion, but think again…

By **NOT** communicating, you make your employees feel undervalued and
underappreciated. And you create questions and churn—the very things you were
trying to avoid.

Effective communication provides the right information, prevents misinformation
and drama, and can engender a sense of pride, commitment, and trust that keeps
employees coming back and giving their best effort. It's also consistent, constant,
and honest.

"Deafness has left me acutely aware of both
the duplicity that language is capable of and
the many expressions the body cannot hide."

– Terry Galloway, Performance Artist

Managing the Company Rumor Mill

All organizations have a rumor mill. It's a natural part of the employee network. And as much as leaders would like to shut it down, they can't. But they can manage it.

Here are five easy strategies for managing the company rumor mill:

Maintain your credibility and use it to your advantage. Credibility won't stop rumors from developing, but it will unleash the truth. Communicate what you know, when you know it, and make sure your messages are consistent across all touch points.

Be open, but be careful. We know that remaining silent in tough times feeds anxiety and fuels the rumor mill. But being too open can hurt more than it helps, especially if it adds to people's fears.

Pulse your people. Ask your direct reports what they're hearing from their people on a periodic basis. Or, better yet, walk the halls and ask employees what's on their minds. Having a better sense of what keeps employees up at night will help you get ahead of any rumors that might be waiting in the wings. The best part is that employees will know you're listening and that you care about what they are thinking.

Anticipate and address concerns. When people are worried about what they don't know, they often imagine the worst and share their concerns with others. If leaders don't anticipate and address concerns, the vacuum will most certainly be filled by rumors. Get out in front of anticipated worries by understanding the mindset that causes them and immediately addressing those concerns.

Include your own messages in the rumor mill. Engage thought leaders who typically feed and influence the rumor mill, along with supervisors throughout the organization. When employees hear the same messages from their supervisor (always their preferred source) or from the CEO, read it on the intranet, and hear it through the rumor mill, they're more likely to believe it and, most importantly, to act on it.

1 2 3 4 **5**

Think about who else can benefit
from your information

At the End of Every Meeting, or When You Make Key Decisions, Ask Yourself:

Who else needs to know this information, how will they get it, and who will get it to them? This ensures that you are keeping others apprised of their need-to-know information and everyone aligned.

TIP:

The effects of a disengaged workforce

Not sure if it's worth it to communicate key pieces of information to people in your company? Consider the following liabilities that stem from a disengaged workforce[11]:

- **More absenteeism.** In a 10,000-person company, absenteeism due to disengagement results in about 5,000 lost days per year, which is valued at $600,000 in salary paid in which there was no work performed.

- **More turnover.** Business units comprised of mostly disengaged employees have 31 percent more turnover than those made up of mostly engaged employees.

- **More theft.** Work groups with high numbers of disengaged employees lose 51 percent more of their inventory.

- **More injuries.** Work groups with engagement scores in the bottom quartile average 62 percent more accidents in the workplace.

- **Lower customer satisfaction scores.** Work groups with higher levels of engagement have 12 percent higher customer scores than those on the lower end.

- **Lower productivity and profitability.** Work groups in the top quartile of engagement are three times more likely to succeed, average 18 percent higher productivity, and 12 percent higher profitability.

Everything a company and its leaders want to accomplish happens through people, making communication a critical business tool and an important differentiator.

TRY IT TODAY

Think about how you can improve communications to engage employees.

- **How well are you listening?** Ask managers what they are hearing; walk around and ask employees what they think; or invite a group to lunch to hear what they have to say.

- **Could you be communicating more mission-critical information?** Is there something you could share but haven't? An opportunity to update that you've avoided? Take the risk and see how much your team appreciates the information.

- **Have you built a word-of-mouth network?** Identify a few leaders in your employee ranks and invite them for a conversation to get acquainted; this will open channels to deliver your messages through word-of-mouth in the future.

The Three Most Common Myths Leaders Believe About Communication Style

Starting thought

What Might You Be Myth-ing?

It's easy to see why there are some common myths around communication. In today's world we see politicians, advertisers, and the media present sound bites and information to convey whatever they want to convey, regardless of its accuracy. The Internet has opened up the world to a constant source of information—24 hours a day, 7 days a week—whether there's "new news" or not. No longer are we in a world of careful research and fact-finding, of accepting information from only trusted sources, of going to a reference source for data. Sadly, it's become a matter of information quantity, not quality.

Our world now is one of accepting whatever is presented to us, of using Wikipedia as a form of data. Being in the communication field, I can tell you that data gathered from a website that is populated by individuals sharing their thoughts and opinions—and saying whatever they want to be true—is not typically reliable information. We are a world that is beginning to accept information first and only challenge it later.

There is a time and place to be skeptical and challenging of ideas, just like there is a time and place to be smart and careful about making assumptions. Believe it or not, the most common myths about communication come from assumptions.

The downside with assumptions is that you might not realize you even hold a certain assumption, or you might see an assumption as a fact because you've never had the opportunity to disprove it.

I have worked with many executives on communication issues that have arisen because of assumptions or myths. When I dispelled the myth and put better practices in place, things got better.

In what ways do you challenge the information you receive?

"Most of our assumptions have outlived their uselessness."

– Marshall McLuhan, Philosopher

MYTH #1

I don't have time to communicate

The most common myth that I hear is, "I don't have time to communicate." The leader perceives that there is not enough time to draft a plan or to communicate a plan. Therefore, more could be done in the time saved from drafting and sharing a plan—no different from the adage, "Clean as you go." We all know it's easier to clean up as you go when cooking—to put things away when you're finished using them, rather than wait until later, or worse, hope it will clean itself up.

Taking the time to communicate, whether up front or at any critical point, will minimize problems, create efficiencies, and perhaps even buy you some time. Strategic communication can minimize the downsides of change in which business can be stopped, slowed, or interrupted, and can maximize the upside of change to accelerate business results.

In a recent change effort for a Fortune 100 client, the first thing we did was to create a plan that would ensure all people and teams involved knew what the outcomes and objectives were, knew who was responsible for what, and knew the deadlines and milestones. We even included a section for tracking progress and planned a section for communicating to everyone on a regular basis. We outlined what was needed in the beginning and how to keep everyone productive, motivated, and 'in the know' as the project moved forward. All good—all the right things to do.

However, once the tactical parts of the plan were put into place, like timelines, the plan as it was could be distributed to everyone and work could start. The part of the plan for communicating through the project had not been completed yet, but the leaders said "No worries, let's get people started so we can get on with things and then we will finish up the communication part of the plan." Guess what happened?

The leaders never got around to finishing that part of the plan and, of course, there was never additional communication to the group after the tactical plan went out to everyone. There was some confusion at first because the plan wasn't explained to everyone, and the folks who didn't understand just checked out or were a problem in the overall project, pushing back, and not acting like team members. As time went on, the folks who had understood what the plan meant and started on it, lost excitement around it. They lost focus. Confusion occurred and stagnation started. As conflicts arose, stalemates started. Focus and effort waned.

By contrast, a little communication at the beginning of a change effort to set the tone—and during it to ensure understanding, agreement, and focus—can make a huge difference. The time you spend communicating will keep problems from happening and will usually reward you by creating more time long-term.

MYTH #2

People won't interpret situations if you don't talk about them

After talking about the downside of assumptions or myths and how they can get in the way of leading effectively, here's the second myth—people won't interpret situations or give them meaning if leaders don't talk about them.

Think of a time when someone has done something to you but they haven't apologized or acknowledged it or said anything to you about it. You then see that person, and it is so awkward, with this "thing" out there like an elephant in the room. Or, it's infuriating, as you are sitting there thinking to yourself, "I can't believe he isn't saying anything about this...he's going to blow this off...he thinks I'm going to just sit here and pretend it didn't happen."

How did you feel? What were you thinking about the person? I imagine...rude, avoidant, trying to pull something over me...yes, those are often our interpretations when someone slights us. But they're just that...interpretations. Now, they may actually be true. We all know the person who did that to us who really is a jerk, so labeling him as a jerk here actually fits!

You can see how we make interpretations, whether right or wrong, no matter the situation. That is human nature. Our brains are wired to interpret information and find meaning in it.

So whether people forget to tell us something or whether people choose not to tell us something...how people communicate is always a choice (whether they intend it or not). When we don't communicate, people will just come up with their own meaning. My mom is learning this slowly. While she still has trouble understanding what I do, she does remember the title to my previous book, *You Can't **NOT** Communicate*, and is working hard to apply the principle.

What might you be communicating that you don't intend to?

MYTH #3

Talking is communication

Here's the last myth—talking is communication. As we know, just because you're talking doesn't mean you're communicating. We all know someone who can talk for hours without saying very much.

There are four critical components or "musts" that help distinguish communicating from talking.

Must No. 1

Understand your audience. You must adjust your message to best match your audience. You can't just share data. That is the difference between a bookkeeper printing out financial reports and handing them over to you, and a controller or CFO interpreting the data into critical information that's relevant and helps guide decisions.

Must No. 2

Engage the listener. Get their respect, interest, and attention. Talk to them, not just to anyone. Use empathy to demonstrate sincerity.

Must No. 3

Be truthful and direct. You have to have respect for people to get them to buy in to your communication. You maintain respect through the integrity of your communication and through the consistency of your words and actions.

One issue that comes up when we talk about the idea of being truthful and direct is the issue of confidentiality and of what is and isn't appropriate to share with different groups or different people. As a leader, you have a duty to keep some things confidential, forever or for a while. An example of this is when layoffs are coming, and leadership is working on it but it isn't time to tell the company or team yet.

Must No. 4

Plan your method for communicating. Email is not always the best way to communicate. Face-to-face, 'live,' is best when communication is about a tough issue or is a tough message. And you can't 'wing it." The Nike slogan, *"Just Do It"* doesn't apply here. You need to be purposeful, which takes planning.

"I therefore claim to show, not how we think in myths, but how myths operate in our minds without our being aware of the fact."

– Claude Levi-Strauss, Philosopher

TRY IT TODAY

Compare your last communication effort to the list of communication "musts."

- **Did you understand your audience and engage them?** Did you adjust your message and communication vehicle to meet their needs? Make a list of the different audiences you worked with and how you could have engaged them or communicated better.

Look ahead to the next communication initiative and create a thoughtful plan.

- **Who is critical to the initiative's success and what is important to them?** Be clear on the perspective of your audience and how to engage them.

- **What does the audience need to know?** While some information may be confidential, be as truthful as you can and help them to see how their efforts link to the business goal.

- **What is the best channel for communication?** Consider which people are affected by the initiative and what vehicle is best for delivering information—several vehicles including e-mail and face-to-face communication may be needed.

SE7EN
DEADLY SINS
OF LEADERSHIP

Bad Habits
That Can Derail

Starting thought

Bad Habits You'll Want to Know About and Avoid

The truth is that most leaders didn't get where they are because of their communication skills. Most often, they were strong individual contributors who achieved business results relating to bottom line and company growth. But now that they're at the top, they need to master the new and challenging skills of engaging and influencing others to connect each and every employee to overarching company goals. They can only go so far on their technical skills and abilities. Those used to be the requirements to get things done. Today, leaders who want to accomplish goals and move a business forward know that can only happen through others.

Before they can engage their teams to achieve success, however, leaders need to be aware of a whole host of bad habits that can derail even the most motivated leader's initiatives. I call these "The Se7en Deadly Sins of Leadership." Oh, yes, they are sins, and they are deadly. In my experience and without exception, I've seen that ineffectual and struggling leaders succumb to one or more of these communication challenges. Alternatively, strong, influential leaders, whether consciously or not, are avoiding these deadly sins to connect with their employees and drive company-wide success.

For most leaders, avoiding any of the Se7en Deadly Sins takes honest self-assessment and a concerted effort. And only by knowing these sins—or common traps that leaders fall into—can you begin to think about how to navigate around them. Only then, as leaders, can we make the greatest impact on the people we lead. With time and practice, good habits replace bad, and your past life of leadership sin becomes a distant memory. The strategies here are proven and I've seen them work irrespective of the industry, economy, or the leader's personality.

What sins do you succumb to, and how are you rising above them?

"Measles are less
contagious than bad habits."

– Mignon McLaughlin, Journalist and Author

SIN 1: MYOPIA

(The sin of only seeing what's right in front of you)

You? The Company's Point Person for Vision, Shortsighted?
Sadly, it's true. Leaders who are great at keeping the big picture in mind and tending to the minutiae of the business are often too focused on managing these pieces to lift their heads to see what the people around them—yes, those employees who are essential to achieving every company goal—are doing, thinking, and feeling. And more important still, while you had your head down, your door closed, or were assuming your team would figure things out by osmosis, they were grasping at the few communications you did share—whether in the form of an email, body language, or a raised voice—to make their own inferences and assumptions about company values and goals.

Is that really what you want?

It's up to you to break out of your own world. To reflect on the message you are sending to your team through your communication—or lack thereof.

Are you purposeful about how you spend your time, what you focus on, who you interact with, the people you recognize, and other actions that send a message?

**Don't let your myopia force others to interpret
and create your message for you...**

TIP:

Innies, take note!
Here's why communication is especially challenging for introverts: introverts think they're communicating more than they are. The quality of their communication is sound, but the quantity is lower than needed.

Outies, take note!
Here's why communication is especially challenging for extroverts: the quantity of their communication is high, but the quality is low. It's common for extroverts to talk a lot without saying much that's meaningful and credible.

Note to self: All of us can be more cognizant of how our style impacts how we communicate, and flex our style to various situations.

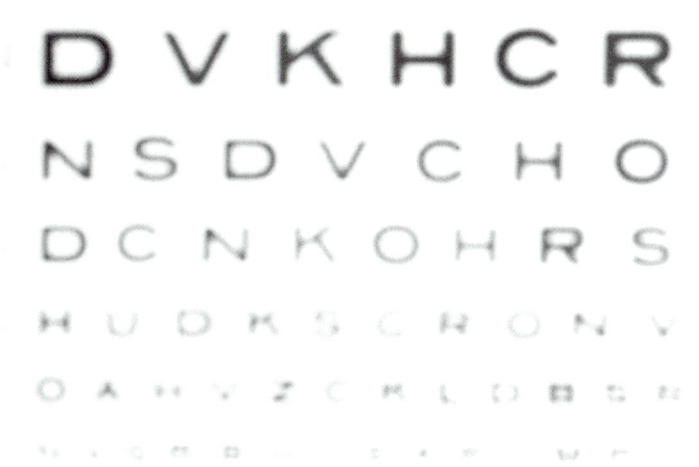

SIN 2: HYPOCRISY

(The sin of failing to practice what you preach)

In a 2006 Zogby Study[12]**, Although 98 Percent of People Surveyed Believed That Honesty and Trust are Most Important in the Workplace, 69 Percent of Respondents Ranked the Trustworthiness of Corporate Leaders as "Low"**

There is a crisis of trust in business today. You can't turn on the TV or read a newspaper without seeing how one leader or another has let his or her integrity—or at least good decision making—slip. These glaring examples of dishonesty may be the extreme, but many leaders compromise trust every day with small sins of Hypocrisy. Nobody wants to be called a hypocrite. But if you're preaching one thing and practicing another…well, there's no getting around the facts.

Most leaders don't mean to be hypocritical, it's just that they often don't see that their own behaviors or words are at odds with the very expectations they have for their employees. But if you're telling your team one thing while doing another, not only is your message unlikely to sink in, you may even engender distrust and hostility among your employees. There's no better way to connect with employees to build trust than by being honest and consistent in your communication and actions.

Leader hypocrisy is all the more likely if leaders aren't willing to surround themselves with their own trusted "truth-tellers." Truth-tellers are colleagues or peers who shed light on company issues and individual leader behaviors not as they should be or as leaders would like to see them, but as they actually are.

Building Trust That Lasts

When people trust you, your ability to persuade them increases exponentially.

Here are tried-and-true strategies that work to build trust:

- Be approachable and friendly (people trust leaders they like).
- Balance the need for results with being considerate of others and their feelings.
- Instead of using your position of power, work hard to win over people.
- Ensure your words and actions match.
- Actively listen and check for understanding by paraphrasing what you've heard.
- Show support for your team members, even when they make mistakes.
- Be honest and tell the truth. Telling people what you think they want to hear erodes trust.

As leaders, we can't underestimate the power of the shadow we cast and, as a consequence, our ability to influence behaviors to drive results.

SIN 3: SLOTH

*(The sin of being too lazy to commit time
and resources to great communication)*

**Now That We've Established That Leaders Are Almost
Always Communicating—Even When They Don't Realize
They Are—It's Fair to Say That 80 Percent to 90 Percent
of the Average Leader's Day is Spent Communicating**

But how much time are those same leaders spending
planning for those communications, and thinking about the
messages that they are sending? More like 10 percent.

It's a fact that leaders are used to putting time and energy into business
plans, product launches, business succession plans, and more, but when
it comes to planning for day-to-day communication, most fall prey to the
third Deadly Sin: Sloth.

**Effective communication is
purposeful, and that takes planning.**

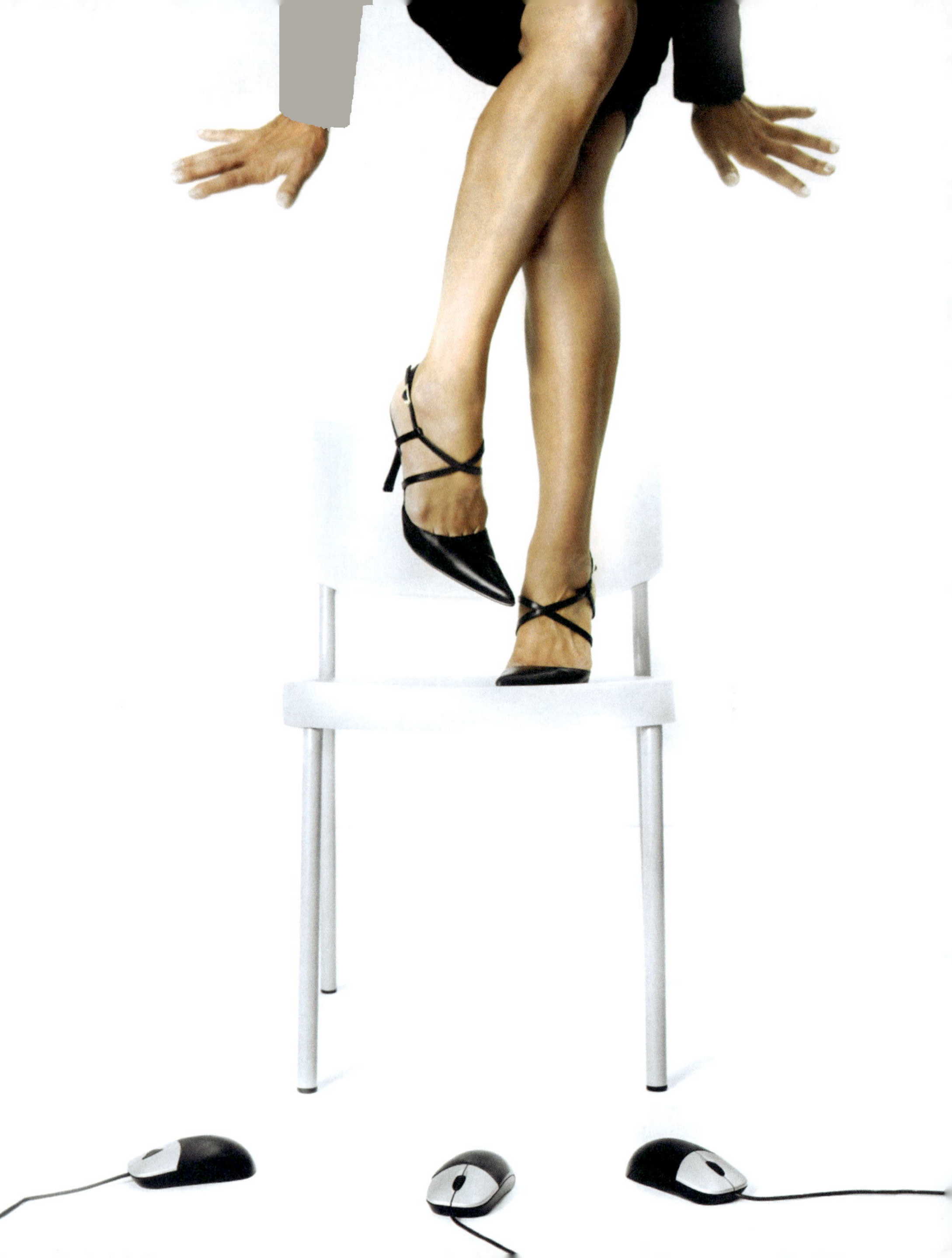

SIN 4: DETACHMENT

*(The sin of being disconnected
and distanced from your team)*

It Sounds So Simple—Employees Follow Leaders Because of How Leaders Make Them *Feel*

Leadership is personal, but in their focus on business goals, leaders often detach themselves from the human element of the workplace, thereby failing to show they care about their team members.

Is Detachment a sin you're guilty of? Ask yourself how well you know your team. What are they passionate about? What are the little things that matter to them? When are their birthdays? When was the last time you interacted with them as people, not simply as your employees? When was the last time you said thank you?

By engaging with team members and employees, leaders have the power to boost morale, engagement, and excitement, and studies have shown that motivated and involved teams are measurably more productive and successful than disengaged teams. People won't listen to you until they know who you are and that you care.

SIN 5:

MATERIALISM

(The sin of finding more value in counting short-term deliverables than in achieving long-term goals)

As a Leader, Are You Output-Focused Instead of Outcome-Focused? Are You Too Focused On a Tree to See the Forest? Then You're Likely a Victim of What I Like to Call "Shiny Object Syndrome." In Terms of our Deadly Sins, This Translates as Materialism

Instead of thinking about end results and achieving goals, leaders often put too much emphasis on the importance of managing individual tasks and projects. Focus on these material, tangible details rather than the big picture leads to the kind of micromanagement that devalues members of your team and distracts from long-term goals and success. When leaders focus on the destination, rather than the minutiae of the road to getting there, they inspire their team while keeping them focused on the common goal.

Want to avoid Materialism and inspire your team? Consider using phrases like, "The outcome we seek on this project is…" or "What's the problem we're trying to solve?"

Leaders and team members won't get lost in the weeds as long as their final destination is always in sight.

SIN 6: PRESUMPTION

*(The sin of assuming that everyone
shares your perspective and understanding)*

Sure, It Makes Sense That You Would First Approach Any Message From Your Point of View. The Trick is Learning How to Get Beyond the Assumption That Everyone Else Shares Your Perspective and Will Perceive Issues the Same Way You Do

Yet this is a common trap that leaders fall into. Because they are so used to leading the discussion, they forget that they may need to adjust communication to fit a specific audience, who might see issues from varying perspectives or have different concerns. This is the sin of Presumption. In short, leaders focus on the message before thinking about where the audience is coming from.

Leaders might like to think that communication is all about simply airing their own ideas; in fact, real communication happens in the mind of the listener. Good leaders understand that audiences differ—there can even be a variety of audience needs within a given team—and that messages must be tailored in a way that speaks to each individual audience. Just as important, the more you know about your audience, the better you'll be able to speak to them in a way that is meaningful for them, thereby influencing and moving them to action.

Only with this kind of connection does real communication happen.

Real communication happens in the mind of the listener.

SIN 7: IRRELEVANCE

*(The sin of failing to provide meaningful context
for project and company goals and objectives)*

Do You Feel Like People in Your Company Are Walking Around With Blinders On? Like Every Project Exists in a Bubble? Like No One Has Any Idea How What They're Doing Fits Into the Grand Scheme of the Company Mission? That's Because Leadership is Guilty of Our Final Deadly Sin: Irrelevance

The bottom line is this: If leaders aren't providing context or relevance for objectives, employees are left to grasp for meaning in the dark.

Employees don't need to know everything, but they do need to know the "WHAT" and the "WHY." What are we doing, and why are we doing it? Without this overarching context, your team lacks the information to work with purpose and direction. Then, your team needs to know how it affects them and what's in it for them.

Next time someone on your team makes a mistake or moves in the wrong direction, take a moment to look at yourself. You may be surprised to discover that you failed to provide context, thereby setting in motion further failures down the line.

When your team makes a mistake, ask yourself: What context didn't I provide them that would have made the difference between a miss and a win?

"A bad habit is something you can do without thinking—which is why most of us have so many of them."

– *Frank A. Clark, Author*

TRY IT TODAY

Take an honest look at your leadership style and assess which of "The Se7en Deadly Sins" may be at work, then make a positive change.

- **Myopia**—How will you change your communication to ensure employees have the right message? Start today.

- **Hypocrisy**—How can you better align your actions and your words? Do it.

- **Sloth**—How can you increase effort and resources devoted to communication? Take action now.

- **Detachment**—How do you make your team feel? Take three steps to become more connected.

- **Materialism**—Are you more focused on outcomes or output? Develop a statement to explain your big-picture goal.

- **Presumption**—Think about your most important current activity and write a statement of what your listeners need to know considering how their perspective differs from yours.

- **Irrelevance**—Write a statement of context to help communicate the company goals and objective in a more meaningful way to your employees.

Two-Way Communication

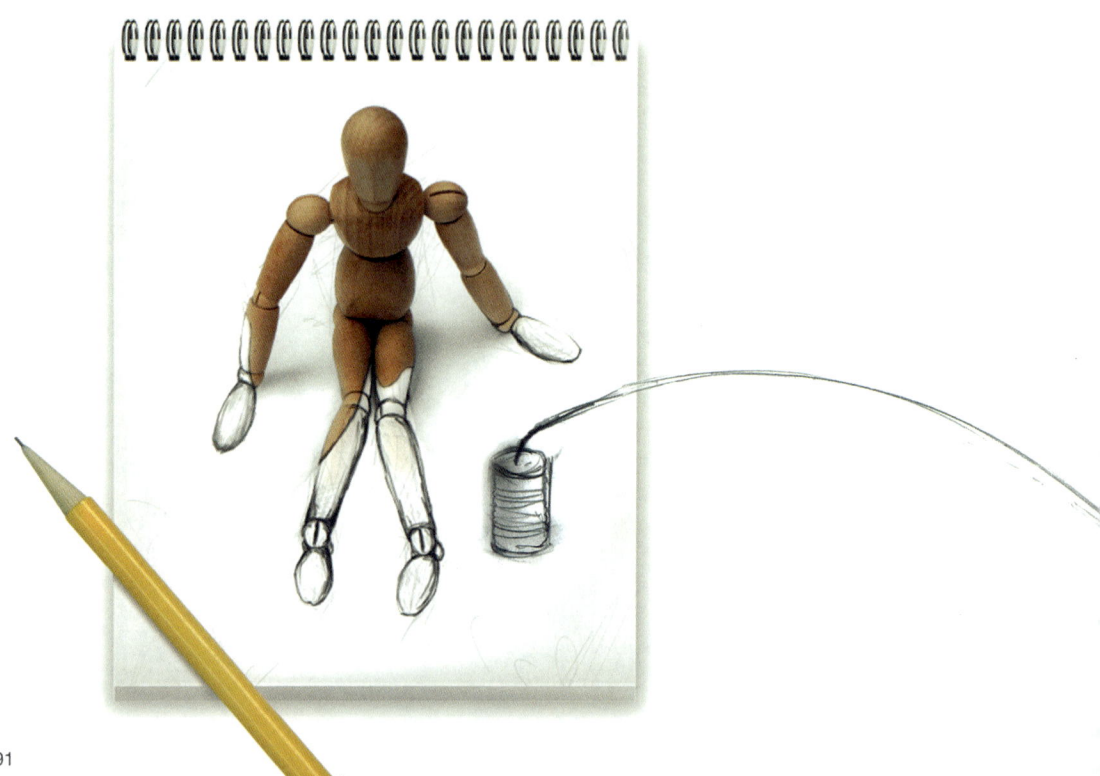

Strategies to Create Conversation and Meaning

Starting thought

The Million-Dollar Question

I used to ask a lot of questions as a kid, which got me into huge trouble with adults. I constantly wondered why things worked the way they did (including us humans). "Enough already with the questions," my mom would say. Like clockwork, she'd shoot back, impatiently, "Ask your father." I never got a straight answer from him, just a pun, which often made me smile or more often, groan.

I may not have known at the time, but now I understand why "why" matters, and the importance of asking questions and getting feedback. Questions drive understanding and smart problem solving. Before you can solve a business problem or achieve a goal, you have to understand what the situation is. Asking questions is the best way to come at a problem from varied perspectives:

- Is this really a problem or just the symptom?
- What else could be behind this? Contributing to this?
- What are the other stakeholders going to ask? Going to be concerned with?

You're limiting your effectiveness if you problem-solve from assumptions or just the information at hand. And, rarely do good leaders have all the answers. Good leaders:

- Ask questions to gather more data and to test the data they have
- Ask questions to get a variety of perspectives
- Engage other smart people in developing the best answers
- Create input mechanisms for frequent, two-way communication

It's a trap in business that leaders think that they should have all the answers or that they do have all the answers. Encouraging dialogue not only helps gather information and ideas that help find answers, it engages employees in the process. Asking questions also serves another important purpose—it helps us know ourselves. Good leaders know that how well we understand ourselves has a profound impact on our ability to navigate in the social realm. In some areas we know ourselves well; in others, we are biased. Part of asking questions also is about getting feedback about yourself; knowing change begins and ends with you.

> How are you doing when it comes to engaging employees in dialogue and asking questions to understand, make smart decisions, and get to know yourself better?

"Two monologues
do not make
a dialogue."

– Jeff Daly, Author

Dos and Don'ts of Effective Two-Way Communication

Want to fast-track your communication effectiveness? Here's how:

DO THIS...	NOT THAT...
Communicate with the audience in mind	Communicate from your perspective
Listen	Talk, talk, talk
Plan your communication	Wing it
Repeat your message	Communicate your message one time
Ask open-ended questions	Tell
Ask for input	Forgo others' perspectives and be out of touch
Share what you know, when you know it	Withhold information or wait until you have all the answers
Know yourself	Be a "stranger" to yourself
Tell the truth	"Spin it"
Create dialogue	Talk "at" people
Seek out information when you don't know it	Make up communication
Check for understanding	Assume you've been understood
Add context and make communication relevant	Simply pass information along
Purposefully seek out diverse opinions	Listen just to those opinions you agree with
Listen for what's not said	Listen for what you want to hear

Twelve Must-Have Skills for Effective Two-Way Communication

It's time to think about the actual skills you need to improve two-way communication.

So just what are these skills? Following is the list of 12 must-know, must-master abilities that make for good communication. There's one for every month of the year, but it won't take you a month to apply each of these skills. Maybe 12 weeks?

You must have an ability to:

1. Select the right time and method for communicating

2. Be present in the moment and limit distractions

3. Provide the big-picture and context first; check for understanding before sharing more detailed information

4. Ask broad, open-ended questions to gather feedback

5. Share the rationale behind decisions

6. Listen for what's being said (and not said)

7. Ask more specific questions to ensure understanding

8. Listen some more (stop talking)

9. Empathize and reflect back feelings when appropriate

10. Check for understanding (paraphrase)

11. Ask for feedback (what's working well/what could be better)

12. Ensure shared understanding/meaning before the conversation ends

In the end, employees will give you credit for trying. Self-disclose by letting them know what you're working on, and ask them how you're doing. It shows you care, and you'll get kudos for trying even when the outcome isn't exactly what you want.

The currency
for business today
is **conversation**

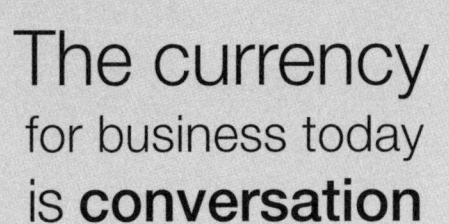

Feedback Channels to Build Dialogue

By establishing channels to encourage and funnel feedback from employees to leaders, you create a critical structure to support employee engagement. Here are some steps to build it:

Understand what's important to your audience

The top priority for building engagement is to give employees information they need to succeed in their jobs, and ensure they know where to find additional resources. The type of organization, job, and level of employee will dictate the most effective channel to meet your needs. Your efforts will be most effective if you first ask yourself, "What is the most important thing these employees want to know, what is the best way to encourage dialogue, and how would they be most comfortable sharing input?"

Choose or create channels

Once you consider the audience and work environment, look at the best ways to engage employees to share their ideas and insights. You may use existing channels or create new ones. Keep in mind feedback channels can be informal—such as leaders "managing by walking around" or supervisors asking for input—or they can be more formal mechanisms that invite ideas and questions in print or via technology. When determining which channels work best, keep in mind employees' time commitment, availability, and access to technology. Be sure they can use feedback mechanisms both during and after work hours.

Respond quickly to feedback

Once you are ready to implement and promote feedback channels throughout the organization, recognize that what you do with their input speaks volumes to employees. When leaders respond quickly to ideas and questions, employees get the message their input is valued and they become more committed and engaged. To ensure feedback gets the respect it deserves, assign someone to respond personally and promptly to all employee concerns and ideas.

Act on feedback

Highly engaged employees are enthused about their organization and believe they can positively influence its success. Acting on employee feedback and highlighting the impact employees make is a strong engagement builder. Be sure that all employees know how their colleagues' suggestions or ideas are being implemented. Regularly sharing results and requesting additional feedback creates predictable, consistent, two-way communication that encourages employees to take ownership and understand their ideas are valued by the organization.

TIP:

The ubiquitous 80/20 rule

What's the right mix of speaking vs. listening at an all-employee or team meeting?

Leaders should listen 80 percent of the time, and share their perspective for about 20 percent. That helps ensure the leader is in learning mode—understanding what's working well, what's not, and most importantly, how things can be better.

Doesn't that beat the "We have all the answers" approach?

Nine Fast (and Not So Fast) Fixes To Poor Two-Way Dialogue

If you're reading this book, the chances are good that you know you can be even better. And that's a good start. All too often, leaders and managers don't even realize they are having communication issues, and that can make an already bad situation even worse.

But if you know you're having problems, you can begin to make the changes that will make a real difference, and the truth is, the changes are not as hard as you might think. We frequently work with our clients on essential must-do strategies for enhancing two-way dialogue, and they are often surprised that these fixes are not as challenging as they first imagined. That's not to say that change happens overnight, but it does mean that with a little attention and self-awareness, everyone has the power to improve their two-way communication.

To improve communication, managers need to:

- Understand their role and the expectations leadership has of them (that means leadership needs to have and articulate expectations)

- Be self-aware so their own issues, challenges, and filters don't get in the way

- Be trained on how to drive two-way communication

- Let their staffs know there's an issue, seek input from them as to how to improve two-way communication (what's working well/what could be better), and then act on their suggestions

- Have a communication plan for their team, which ensures a regular cadence of opportunities to have dialogue about the state of the business, results, how the team is doing, the impact of decisions on the team, and so on

- Be held accountable for those expectations and behaviors

- Share their expectations of staff when it comes to communication

- Regularly ask their teams how communication is flowing (what's working well/what could be better), and then act on those suggestions

- Measure the state of communication regularly (a survey once a year isn't enough)

I'm Not Kidding: Three Steps To Be a Better Listener

At a recent kid's story time event at the local bookstore, I overheard its storyteller with directions for the toddlers.

"Before we get started, what do we need to do?" she asked in her kid-friendly voice, reminding attendees of the rules of story time (complete with helpful gestures perfect for the 2- to 4-year olds and their parents).

Together, they all said:

Open your ears... Close your mouth... Eyes on me

Brilliant, I thought. These three strategies can work for anyone who needs to listen, or who wants to improve their listening skills. It's amazing that much of what we learn as kids can translate to the workplace, and often how quickly we forget simple but powerful principles that could make life at work a whole lot better.

Make the Grade with the Four Fs of Feedback

The ability to give meaningful feedback is at the heart of all good face-to-face communication. Without an honest assessment of performance—whether good or bad—you are limiting or undercutting the value of every interaction, and you are most certainly falling short as a leader and failing to help your employees evolve and develop.

If you were to give yourself a grade for how effective you are at giving feedback, what grade would you choose? Many leaders are brutally honest and give themselves an F. They realize that they don't make giving feedback a standard part of meetings and discussions. They give general praise ("Good job!") versus specific feedback ("Here's what you did extremely well on this project…"), and they often don't give feedback at all or wait so long to give it that it does little good for the person receiving it.

The truth is that most of us would be significantly more effective at work if we gave others feedback sooner and more regularly. It helps all of us work better. It helps us to recognize blind spots, know what to keep doing (and when to think about changing specific behaviors), and it helps build relationships with those who give us the gift of their advice.

Although we all might like to blame the challenges of giving feedback on external circumstances, the biggest barrier to giving feedback is often ourselves. It is difficult for most of us to offer criticism when we are looking someone in the eye. We're concerned about how a person will react. At the same time, we want to minimize conflict or protect our ego. Both lead to postponing the conversation or not having it at all.

However, feedback is best given within a face-to-face context, as it is most likely to be well received and acted upon. When sitting down with an employee in person, we are better able to respond, coach, and teach to his or her defensiveness, to mitigate criticism with recognition of achievements, and to give someone time to absorb the message. There is simply no substitute for personal interaction when it comes to imparting honest feedback.

The Four Fs

When you're ready to give feedback, timing matters. First, choose a time when you are at your best, and in the right frame of mind, so that there's the greatest chance that your comments will be heard, understood, and appreciated in the spirit that they're meant. Your credibility as a leader is at stake. Once you're ready, ask the other person if they're open to hearing what you have to say. If so, proceed. If not, schedule a follow-up. Either way, offering a choice gets you off on the right foot (but don't let them off the hook if they're not ready; be persistent and let them know that you have an important message for them that affects how they work).

Once you pick the right time, here are the "Four Fs of Feedback" to help you move your grade from an F to an A:

1.
Frame

Set up the discussion and provide context as to why you're sharing feedback, including your motivation and intent. Most often, your intention is to be helpful, and it's critical to say that to establish a positive context for the discussion. As you might expect, when employees are on the defensive, they are less likely to respond to and act on the comments. Here's what a good approach might sound like: "I need to share some feedback with you. Are you open to that right now? My intention is for this to be helpful to you and for you—and us—to be more effective. If it were me, I would want to receive this feedback."

2.
Feedback

Discuss what went well or what could be better, and suggest an alternative. Feedback should never be personal; discuss a specific behavior and then the consequence. For example, "This behavior had this consequence, and here's what I'd prefer to see…" Avoid emotionally charged language or judgments, and just state the facts as they are.

3.
Feelings

Check to see how effectively you're communicating by creating a two-way dialogue. A simple "How do you feel about what I just said?" gives a person permission to respond and to share their impressions and understanding—and any context that you might not know about that might explain their behavior. Let them respond without interruption, then clarify or amplify if needed.

4.
Follow-up

Discuss specific next steps and how you can help. This is also your chance to help your staff understand that feedback has become an important part of your leadership style, and that you're fostering an environment in which it will become common. Make sure they understand feedback is a two-way street, and that you expect them to feel comfortable sharing it and other ideas in the spirit of continuous improvement. Of course, this means you must demonstrate the same behaviors when receiving feedback that you expect of your people when you give it.

Being timely and direct are essential for success. Add a little humanity and caring, and you have a recipe for successfully giving feedback that will build valued, trusting relationships.

What Gets In the Way
Four key issues can hurt your overall effectiveness as a leader, in particular when you need to give feedback.

Emotion. Feeling or being emotional will affect the delivery of your message and might cause your listener to shut down.

Ambiguity. A lack of clarity often causes others to make assumptions and may lead to unnecessary fear or worry.

Time. Feeling pressed for time might mean that you go too fast when giving feedback, do not listen, or mishear important details, all of which can lead to ineffective communication or misunderstanding.

Stress. Being stressed affects your ability to deliver your message in a direct, non-threatening, and helpful way.

If you're receiving feedback, falling into one or more of these four traps might prevent you from embracing the feedback you receive and understanding its true intention. By avoiding these pitfalls or just by being aware of them, you are in a better position to be open to feedback and to avoid misinterpretation and overreaction.

Listen Up! Strategies That Work

Here are some easy steps to demonstrate active listening:

Approach each dialogue with the goal to learn something and think of the person as someone who can teach you.

Stop talking and focus closely on the speaker. Suppress the urge to multitask or think about what you are going to say next.

Open and guide the conversation with broad, open-ended questions such as "How do you envision..." or "What other strategic alternatives did you consider?"

Drill down to the details by asking direct, specific questions that focus the conversation, such as "Tell me more about...," "How would this work?" or "How did you come to this conclusion?"

Summarize what you're hearing and ask questions to confirm your understanding, such as "If I'm understanding you..." or "Tell me if this is what you're saying...."

Encourage with positive feedback. If a speaker lacks confidence or has some trouble expressing a point, encourage them with a nod, a smile, or a positive question to show your interest.

Listen for total meaning. Recognize that, in addition to what is being said, the real message may be non-verbal or emotional; seek true understanding and be sure to respond with empathy.

Pay attention to your responses. Be aware of your body language and recognize that the way you respond to a question is also part of the dialogue. Keep an open mind and show respect for the other person's point of view even if you disagree with it.

TRY IT TODAY

Evaluate where you are using dialogue effectively and how you could expand the lines of communication.

- **How open are you to receiving feedback?** In what ways and through what channels do you invite employee input? Ask for feedback regularly.

- **What are your face-to-face feedback habits?** Practice giving and receiving feedback to improve your communication and make it a way of working. Extend it to your team with a training session that includes role-play and identify a few questions to use and answer regularly.

Mastering the Art of Messaging

Words That Work |

Starting thought

Messaging That Matters Requires a Standard Approach

In today's competitive environment, the pressure is mounting for leaders to find the answers, and inform, inspire, and engage their people—no easy task when employees are busier than ever and feeling more and more disconnected from their organization. Hidden in these tough times is a defining moment for leaders to create real, meaningful connections with their workforce to maintain—if not drive—productivity.

It's a time for leaders to become leader**communicators** and paint a picture of what's possible so employees can see themselves in that picture and deliver on the goals you have.

Great messages aren't the result of momentary inspiration or a rogue creative genius. They're the product of a comprehensive vision that encompasses leadership insights, employee needs, company priorities, and business goals.

However, more often than not, organizations don't apply the same rigorous discipline to planning strategic messages that they would to other areas of the business like operations, finance, or sales and marketing. The result is:

- Different leaders saying different things about the same topic
- Communication tools that have been developed to announce a specific program, initiative, or change, containing different messages
- Creating organizational messages by yourself
- Developing messages on the fly for nearly every program, initiative, or change in the organization

The solution is simple in concept, yet often challenging in execution. To create messaging that matters, you need to take the time and forethought to develop it strategically and communicate it powerfully.

How might you be even more effective with a standard approach to how you develop messages that motivate, inspire, and engage?

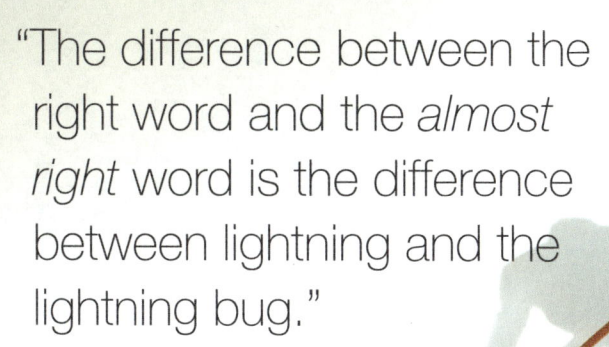

"The difference between the right word and the *almost right* word is the difference between lightning and the lightning bug."

– *Mark Twain*

The Spoils of War (Room)

I remember one specific experience from my time as the director of communications at McDonald's. I was sitting in a "war room" with external communications peers and various leaders and subject matter experts representing a number of functional areas, and together we were planning the communications for an issue that was then affecting the Golden Arches. We came together in a smart, thoughtful, and incredibly efficient way.

We talked about the situation, discussed the facts, weighed options, and mapped the messages and communication approach so that when we left the room a few hours later, we were in lock-step and each leader could go on and deliver their piece of the plan.

I recall thinking, "Why don't we take the same proactive approach to all key internal issues we want to drive through the organization?" I couldn't understand why we weren't using the same smart process and working with the same sense of urgency to help employees understand the company strategy and move them to action. After all, effective communication is known to improve engagement, productivity, and performance.

I knew there had to be a better way…and there is!

Birth of the messagemap™

It's with this principle in mind that I developed our message**map** methodology—a strategic, methodical approach to developing a core message platform that can be delivered in a clear, credible, consistent way.

And it's emerged over the years as a must-have, trusted communication tool for leaders across levels, functions, and industries.

Key indicators that you need a core message platform:
- You need to develop multiple communications, all on the same topic.

- There isn't alignment on what needs to be said about a specific project, initiative, etc.

- You need to communicate a specific topic to different audiences.

- Multiple individuals will be communicating on a specific topic.

The Power of a Process

There's power in having a process that you use consistently to develop key messages and tell your story because it can be done more efficiently and get to higher-impact messages…which ultimately deliver a greater outcome.

THE BOTTOM LINE:

EVERY ORGANIZATION SHOULD
HAVE A STRATEGIC MESSAGING METHODOLOGY

But what is a strategic messaging methodology and what can it do for you, your leaders, and your organization?

Simply put, it's a process that helps you think strategically about how you develop your story, drive alignment, and tell it powerfully—whether it's a large organizational story or whether you want to communicate change inside your organization. When done well, the process allows you to:

- **Define and prioritize the audiences** who will receive the messages and focus on the common ground between them.

- **Identify where key audiences are coming from** and what their information needs are so the messages can influence and drive appropriate action.

- **Agree on and articulate clear, credible, and compelling messages** about the topic.

- **Outline behaviors and actions expected** of key audiences.

- **Connect with your audiences** so they know you and what's important to you.

- **Deliver your messages with confidence** because you're well prepared, know your messages will hit the mark, and you can re-use your platform time and time again to master your delivery.

- **Validate the implementation plan** on a topic and identify any gaps before going "prime time."

A messaging methodology helps you efficiently capture the core messages for any kind of topic—organizational, key initiatives, timely announcements, department plans, even people—in a strategic message platform, like the message**map**.

Your strategic message platform is the foundation for all communication relating to a particular topic. Think of it as the blueprint from which you build customized communications to reach your end audience (e.g., employees, clients, customers, etc.) so they're getting the information in a way that meets their needs.

Examples of communication tools that can be developed using components of a message platform include:

- Management talking points
- Marketing collateral (e.g., brochures)
- Speeches
- Voicemail and email messages
- Web site copy
- Blog copy

- Social media applications
- FAQs
- Press releases
- Direct mail
- Pocket cards
- Presentations

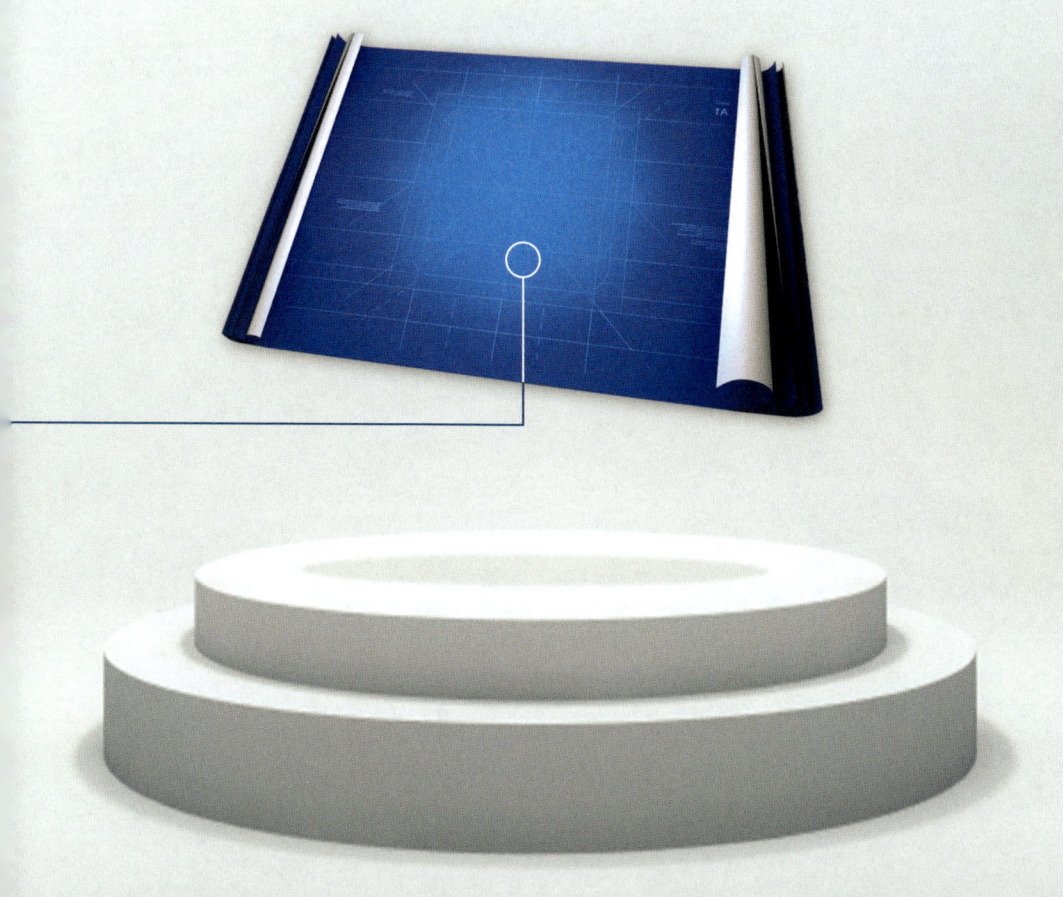

We've talked about what a strategic message platform is. Let's be clear about what it isn't.

A strategic message platform is not:

- **A communication vehicle in and of itself.** Just as an architect wouldn't send the raw design specs to a client to show them what their new house will look like, you don't want to send the message platform on its own, because it will most likely lead to confusion and misunderstanding. Messages should be targeted to resonate with the specific audience.

- **Just the key messages.** A message platform includes data and facts that support and legitimize your main messages, as well as stories that help bring those messages to life.

- **Created and used only by communicators.** The individuals who help you develop the messages also are the individuals who will be talking about the specific topic the most—it's important to ensure they have the key messages and are integrating them into their communication.

- **Static.** Companies evolve, initiatives change, and messages must evolve and change with them to ensure key audiences are getting the information they need.

- **All-purpose.** Once a message platform has been developed, it can be customized for a specific audience to target communication for even greater effectiveness.

- **For one-time use.** A consistent drumbeat of the same messages through different channels and from different voices is the best way to drive your audiences to action; use the messages regularly to ensure the right information is communicated on an ongoing basis.

Know Your Audience

As you develop your message platform, keep your target audiences top of mind. Understand who your key audiences are, where they're coming from on a particular topic, what their information needs are, and what kinds of questions they may ask.

At the same time, also consider what it is you want those audiences to know, how you want them to feel, and what actions you want them to take.

Have these insights ready when creating your message platform because you want the messages to meet your audience's needs. It's the best way to help them get what you're saying, believe in it, and want to act on it.

Think. Feel. Do.[13]

Creating an emotional connection is the fastest way to move someone to action. What do you want your audience to think? How do you want your audience to feel? What do you want your audience to do?

The Makings of a Great Message Platform

Every message platform should start with a main message—*or elevator speech*—that's supported by additional messages, data, and stories that reinforce specific components of the main message.

The main message should summarize a topic at the 40,000-foot level and be able to be delivered in seven to 10 seconds (imagine a short elevator ride from the third floor to the sixth floor).

A great main message:

- Provides a brief snapshot of the topic and what's happening

- Is aspirational in tone

- Can be easily remembered and repeated (it should roll off the tongue and be free of jargon)

- Leaves your audience saying, "Tell me more"

The "tell me more" part comes with the supporting messages, which are the next level of what you need to communicate. The main message won't cover every detail or answer every question your key audience may want to know, which is why the supporting messages are so important.

To amplify your main message, think about the key elements that make up your story and ask some tough questions around:

- What's happening and why is it critical?
- What does "success" look like (the end state)?
- What's new and different?
- What are the benefits to key audiences?
- What's expected of key audiences?

A Story is Worth a Thousand Data Points

Using data, information, and illustrative stories are critical because they answer, "prove it to me," which many audiences will want to know (or are at least thinking about).

This section of your message platform brings your story to life, and reinforces what's important through specific proof points, examples, testimonials, and specific stories that describe the "why," "what," "how," and "what's in it for me."

Consider your key audiences here and where they're coming from. If you're reaching analytical, numbers-oriented people, you'll want data. If you're reaching people who prefer not to get bogged down in the details, illustrative stories may work better.

A story is worth a thousand data points. People remember stories better than any data chart. Use stories to reinforce your point and the behaviors and actions you want to drive.

When it comes time to structuring your message platform—and putting it on paper—know that there isn't just one way to do it. It can be organized in a variety of ways based on what suits you.

The best message platforms:

- Fit on one page (so messages are focused and prioritized)

- Are easy to read and easy to identify the key components of your messages

- Should guide readers through the hierarchy of messages so they understand the topic at a high level before drilling down into the details of the supporting messages, data, and stories

- Factor in how your organization "thinks" (e.g., if your organization is visual in how it presents information, then your message platform could be too)

Identify the Key Players

Message platforms aren't created in a vacuum. You need the people who best know the program or initiative for which you're creating messages.

Think through who else may need to be part of the message platform development so you can engage them in the right way and at the right times. For example, if you're looking to others to help you deliver the messages, let them be a part of developing the messages and hold a messaging session together. Consider how best to tap others for data and stories to bring your messages to life.

Get Ready, Get Set...Then Communicate!

Wait! Don't start developing any communication tools until your audiences are identified, your message platform is developed, and key leaders and subject matter experts are aligned. You'll save time, energy, and rounds of revisions—plus you'll have smarter, higher-impact messages—as a result.

Once your message platform is finalized, then you—or anyone on your team, for that matter—can develop the specific communication tools and tactics needed to drive awareness and action with consistency...everything from emails, voicemails, key talking points for leaders, speeches, brochures, newsletter articles, video scripts, and more.

HINT:
"Test" your messages by running them by a few employees to see how they react. Don't just run it by the agreeable types either. If you can test drive it with someone who may be more cynical and help them understand what you're saying, you know your messages are on the right track.

"Think like a wise man
but communicate in the
language of the people."

– William Butler Yeats

TRY IT TODAY

Think about the most business-critical task you are working on and what messages you want to deliver.

- **Do you have a message platform?** If so, how is it being shared and used? Review it and share it with leaders so they communicate consistently within the organization.

- **Who are the key people with a need to know?** Be sure to prioritize the audiences and outline their information needs so your communication can be most effective.

- **What is your elevator speech?** Summarize your main message in seven to 10 seconds, providing a brief snapshot that can be easily remembered and shared by others.

- **What are your core messages?** Identify the essential points that are appropriate for all audiences and communication vehicles.

- **What details do managers, employees, and customers need to know?** Build out their specific messages with more data, benefits, and expectations depending on the audience and goal.

Advanced Communication Mastery

Taking Fundamentals
to the Next Level

Starting thought

Courage

It's a little-discussed term in business today, yet is at the very core of dealing with the tough situations many leaders face.

I was working with a leader who was preparing to make some significant changes in his organization's structure, including people changes. As we talked more, and his eyes welled up with tears, I realized how tough these decisions were for him. In the end, it was the right thing to do—his customers' needs had changed; the market had changed, and his organization wasn't set up for success.

Through our conversation, he was realizing how difficult this announcement was going to be. In many ways, this was a leadership litmus test—whether he had the courage to not just make a tough decision, but to communicate it with empathy, respect, and sensitivity.

We talked about how he could be authentic about his feelings while still providing the leadership needed to paint a picture of a new future and deliver some difficult messages:

- Clarity would be critical (what is happening and why).
- Courage is needed to be direct and straightforward.
- Compassion and care are vital in communicating how difficult but necessary the changes are.
- Creating a conversation about current and future plans.

In the end, the changes were accepted as well as could be expected. As important, his team got an even better sense of this leader who showed great compassion and courage.

In many ways, his ability to communicate effectively was integral to leading and managing change.

He's someone you'd want to work for in a heartbeat. And his advanced communications skills make the difference.

What courageous conversation might you need to have today and how can you develop your communications skills to prepare?

"Courage is what it takes to stand up and speak; courage is also what it takes to sit down and listen."

— *Winston Churchill*

Embrace Conflict and Transform Discomfort

It's a paradox that every leader faces: create teams that work well together but embrace conflict. Also, drive consensus but encourage individual points of view.

Discomfort is emotional. Feelings can be complex and multi-layered. But stifling expression can inhibit a team's performance and lead to poor decision making.

Here are the top six strategies to drive discomfort for better decision-making:

1. **Make "disagreers" part of your team** (but not disruptors).

2. **Maximize team diversity** to reap the benefits of differences in experience and thinking. Ensure you have various points of view represented at the table.

3. **Encourage debate**, but avoid endless disagreement. Before you make a decision, ensure you have all the points of view on the table. Leave room for passion.

4. **Take on sacred cows**, and allow others to do the same.

5. **Consider alternatives**. Strategic decision-making is about making choices. To make the best choice, you need alternatives.

6. **Always debrief** in the spirit of continuous improvement. Institutionalize the questions, "What worked well?" and "What could we have done better?"

The Most-Forgotten Component of Effective Communication

We're good at communicating the "what." After all, we almost always have a sense of what we want to say. Where we typically miss the mark is the "why:" what's the rationale behind this decision?

When preparing to communicate the "why," think past, present, and future.

"The decision was made because of (past/present) so we can (future)."

For example: "We're starting Casual Fridays because of the overwhelming feedback we received in the employee survey (past/present) as we strive to create a more responsive culture that is better synced with the needs of our workforce (future)."

Influencers Can Help Implement Change and Make it Stick

We've all been there. You've spent months—or even years—developing a new program, strategy, or initiative. It's based on solid research, best practices, company goals, and employee needs. Logically, you cannot think of a single reason your new program should fail. And yet, we all know that in reality the success of implementing anything new depends on a whole lot of intangibles, with none carrying more sway than people's willingness to embrace the new. You can have the best product or program in the world, but if you can't get your audience on board, you're not going to have any luck.

What can you do?

To garner that must-have support, look to one of the most common overlooked audiences: key influencers. These are the movers and shakers from whom others take their cues. With them as your champions, you're guaranteed a serious boost.

Key influencers can help you raise awareness about a business priority, build support throughout the organization, and communicate important messages—the why, what, how, and what's next—to a broader internal audience.

But first, you need to identify them and convince them.

Influencers can help you substantially accelerate the progress of your initiative, or easily get in your way and put a halt to your efforts. Look at influencers as your potentially toughest, but one of the most critical, audiences. If you can convince them, your initiative is bound to succeed because they're your first litmus test. They're going to ask the tough questions they know others will ask. After all, their credibility and reputation (not to mention influence) are on the line.

For best results, ensure you select champions wisely, seek their input, train them, and then equip them with the core communication tools they can use to dialogue with their peers or other audiences. Useful tools might include a master presentation, a one-page visual executive summary, and a frequently asked questions guide.

Align Actions with Words

A leader's ability to inspire and motivate employees is based on trust. When people trust you, they have confidence in your decisions. Even in uncertainty, they will be influenced by your leadership. That is because they expect you to do what you say you'll do.

According to research, 55 percent of employees say that what leaders say and do has the most impact on their perception of an organization[14]. When there is a disconnect between a leader's words and actions, employees are less likely to become engaged and committed to the organization. Actions matter most if you want to earn employees' trust and engage them in the organization. Starting with the leader, it takes involvement at every level to create a deep bond of believability that motivates employees to put forth effort needed to make their organization successful.

Here are some ways that leaders at all levels can build trust by aligning actions with words:

Recognize that building trust takes hard work. Trust must be earned. It comes from a conscious effort to walk your talk, keep your promises, and align your behavior with your values. Building trust is worth the effort because once trust is lost, it can be very difficult to recover.

Be consistent. Consistently doing what you say you'll do builds trust over time—it can't be something you do only occasionally. Keeping commitments must be the essence of your behavior, in all relationships, day after day and year after year.

Be honest and supportive. Even when it's difficult, tell the truth and not just what you think people want to hear. Understand what employees need to know and communicate facts while being considerate of their effort and sensitive to their feelings. Showing support and understanding for your team members, even when mistakes are made, goes a long way in building trusting relationships.

Commit to follow through. Even the best-intended talk is hollow if not followed by corresponding action. Say you'll do something only if you are able to follow through, and don't commit if there is a chance you won't be able to deliver. Breaking a commitment can destroy trust you've built as well as make people less inclined to trust you in the future.

Model the behavior you seek. Nothing speaks more loudly about the culture of an organization than the leader's behavior, which influences employee action and has the potential to drive their results. If you say teamwork is important, reinforce the point by collaborating across teams and functions. Give credit when people do great work and you'll set the stage for an appreciative culture.

Build in accountability. When you and other leaders acknowledge your mistakes as well as successes, employees see you as credible and will follow your lead. You can encourage honest dialogue and foster accountability by building in processes that become part of the culture, such as an evaluation of every project (positives, negatives, things to change) or a status report and next steps in each meeting agenda (tracking deadlines and milestones).

Top 10 Must-Do Strategies for Persuasive Presentations
Prepping for an important presentation? As with any
communication vehicle, purposeful planning is key
to delivering the right message and engaging your
audience with a presentation.

Think about the following 10 criteria for success to help you turn any presentation into a great conversation, and get what you want in record time:

1. Frame communication

- Discuss the purpose of the communication up front.

2. Audience focus

- Communicate with the audience in mind.
- Demonstrate you understand the audience's mindset.

3. Content

- Demonstrate your understanding of the content, including understanding of the business and case for change.

4. Organization

- Present in a clear and well-organized fashion.
- Build in breaks/pauses to check for understanding in a purposeful way (questions are purposefully built-into the presentation to confirm understanding and create dialogue).

5. Tools

- Use visuals appropriately to support the message.

6. Messaging

- Cover core messages clearly and tailor them to the audience.

7. Context

- Discuss and emphasize the rationale.

8. Relevance

- Customize and make messages relevant to the audience (how the audience contributes/fits in).

9. Dialogue/Check for understanding

- Ask questions to clarify others' points of view.
- Ask questions to ensure messages were understood.
- Support honest expression of others' points of view.
- Express reactions and opinions without intimidating others.
- Create a clear structure and process to encourage open exchange of information and viewpoints.
- Minimize distractions during the presentation.
- Express oneself effectively.

10. Presentation style

- Be yourself.

When you practice your presentation, have several colleagues listen and give you feedback on the Top 10 criteria above, and how you did. Then, incorporate their feedback and practice again.

Danger! Differing Definitions Lead to Communication Missteps

Leaders often use concepts such as "competitive," "productivity," and "efficiency," assuming that others share the same definition they do.

These are common concepts for a typical strategic plan, and the basis of critical strategies and actions inside organizations. The reality is that we communicate from our perspective and others hear from their perspective. What's more, we often mistakenly think that others think how we do, rather than being aware of and appreciating the differences among people. We often think more differently than alike. That's why it's critical to define even the most common terms so we can communicate how we—as leaders—see them in the context of our organizations.

Don't assume nodding heads means agreement when you communicate. Define key terms to reduce the chance for confusion. And check for understanding by asking clarifying questions. That way, everyone knows what "efficiency" means and can help you get there.

When More is Less

The higher you are in an organization and/or the more power you have, the less feedback you typically receive.

In actuality, you need more feedback to be successful. That's why smart leaders at all levels surround themselves with "truth tellers" and ask a lot of questions to solicit feedback. Without feedback, leaders might as well be operating in a mirage.

Your questions might be:
- How are we doing at (achieving this goal)?
- What drives you crazy around here?
- Give me three things I do that serve us well.
- Give me three ways in which I can be a better leader.

Ask. Listen. Probe for specifics. Check for understanding. Then, thank the employee for their input. When you use their suggestion, give them credit for their input. That will encourage further suggestions and be a credibility-booster for you. When you don't implement their feedback, explain the rationale behind your decision, and what you considered as alternatives.

TIP:

Here's a strategy that works to check for clarity with concepts that are critical in your organization and with your team:

- Write down the key terms you use most frequently; think about your team's vision, values, key priorities, and so on.

- In your next staff meeting, ask your team what those words mean to them.

- Achieve alignment among your team.

- After the exercise, have someone create your own dictionary of definitions.

TRY IT TODAY

Think about the many perspectives in your organization and how you could harness them to be more effective.

- **Who can look at all sides of an issue?** Identify the "disagreers" who bring different perspectives and aren't afraid to share them. Think of two ways to engage them in adding diverse points of view to team problem-solving.

- **How can influencers help?** Find the key employee influencers in each department or level. Ask their input on your next presentation or challenge and set the stage for later enlisting their help in spreading key messages through the organization.

- **Is everyone speaking the same language?** Be sure leaders and employees are interpreting concepts and words the same way to best achieve common goals. Make a list of important terms and definitions you typically use, and ask employees for their thoughts at your next staff meeting. Clarify where needed to get everyone on the same page.

Communicating with Millennials

Motivating the *Next* "Next Generation"

"The young do not know enough to be prudent, and therefore they attempt the impossible—*and achieve it,* generation after generation."

– Pearl S. Buck, Novelist

Starting thought

Millennial: Phone Home

I have a rising star in my office who happens to be a Millennial. True to form, she's incredibly technologically literate. When I have a computer issue or need to understand the latest social media trend, she's my teacher and coach. Like others in her generation, she's also very open to feedback even though one could perceive her sometimes cocky confidence to mean she's close-minded. She's not at all.

We had a coaching conversation recently about a piece of new-fangled technology we use at The Grossman Group called the telephone, and how every communication can't be an IM or email. Sometimes, I told her, you need to reach out and call someone. Technology has always been part of her life, and it's very much second-nature to her. What's less ingrained is how to pick the right method for various types of communication. That's not just a challenge she faces, but one facing many of the leaders with whom we work.

To engage Millennials—like a member of any audience—you need to understand where they're coming from and what motivates them. The ideas and values they hold are neither good nor bad; they just are. In many cases, Millennials think very differently about the work world than someone from Generation X or the Baby Boomer generation. We can learn a lot from them; they can learn from us.

As the public service message on NBC says, "The more you know….." (Shooting star).

> How are you trying to understand the Millennials on your team or in your organization?

The Next *"Next"* Generation

More than 80 million strong[15], Millennials—those born roughly between 1981 and 2000—are entering the workplace in growing numbers. Just 23 percent of the workforce in 2009[16], they are expected to account for more than 40 percent by 2015[17] and as the estimated 54 million Baby Boomers reach retirement, Millennials will inevitably have even greater impact on organizations.

As it has with every "next generation," the entry of Millennials into the workplace is likely to involve some adjustment. The leader's role is to leverage the talents of all age groups for the greatest competitive advantage. Understanding how they think, work, and communicate—as well as how they relate to one another—is important to achieving that goal.

Whatever their age, the more employees feel understood and valued, the more productive and engaged they are. On the flip side, if they feel misunderstood, it can lead to lower productivity or even disengagement. Millennials are no exception. To better connect with this powerful segment of the workforce, leaders must understand Millennials and how to draw on their unique talents.

What Makes Millennials Tick

Like any generation, there are certain cultural experiences that affect the way Millennials see the world. Baby Boomers grew up watching man walk on the moon, the Vietnam War and the Civil Rights movement. Millennials were shaped by events including the 9/11 terrorist attacks, ethics scandals, and a digital revolution.

A variety of characteristics are commonly seen in this generation. Millennials tend to be socially-minded, technology-literate, confident, and team-oriented. They grew up in an era of choices—whether it was hundreds of television channels, crayon boxes with 96 colors or multi-colored iPods and cell phones. As a result of having so many options all their lives, Millennials value flexibility and convenience more than previous generations. Their experience in group settings such as daycare and after-school sports has also shaped the way Millennials learn and interact. After working with peers throughout their lives, they learn best through collaborative efforts.

Millennials are already shaping the future of many industries and their impact will only grow. Understanding how to tap their talents will benefit every team and organization.

TIP:
Four things you need to know about Millennials:

1. **They are change agents.** Don't expect Millennials to be comfortable with the current workplace "status quo." They thrive in evolving environments and generate change by continuously looking for ways to improve their work with a pioneering mindset. Few Millennials expect to stay with the same organization for many years.

2. **They are technologically sophisticated.** Millennials are comfortable leveraging new digital tools and using technology in new ways. They adapt quickly, so they are good candidates to pilot new processes and help streamline technological transitions to maximize business results. Having Millennials on your team will help your organization roll out new business technologies successfully.

3. **They embrace diversity.** One of the most racially and ethnically diverse generations in business today, Millennials are naturally prepared for globalization. Their approach as part of a global workforce is to offer new ideas and perspectives. As businesses grow, Millennials will be eager and well-suited to contribute because they are both comfortable with and inspired by diversity.

4. **They flourish in a challenging environment.** Millennials enjoy working to their highest potential. When encouraged and coached properly, with regular feedback and opportunities to grow, Millennials will be motivated contributors to your business success.

Millennials at Work

Since the first step to leveraging talent is to understand how people like to work, it is important to recognize that Millennials are:

1. **Focused on results.** They learn by doing and like frequent encouragement and feedback, often seeking ways to develop and improve the quality of their work. They welcome constructive counsel that will help them reach their potential.

2. **True digital natives.** As the first generation to grow up in the information age, Millennials rely heavily on technology to communicate, 24/7. This means they can often benefit from more practice using verbal communication skills in business situations. As leaders, we can teach them about the benefits of face-to-face communication and tap them to help our organizations navigate new technologies.

3. **Great multi-taskers.** Accustomed to focusing on many things at once, Millennials tend to be good at juggling multiple tasks and projects. With this skill, leaders can consider them flexible team members who can successfully handle several responsibilities at the same time.

"Every generation renews itself in its own way; there's always a reaction against whatever is standard."

– Sol LeWitt, Artist

Comparing the Generations

Generation Birth Years	Traditionalists 1922-1945	Boomers 1946-1964	Gen Xers 1965-1980	Millennials 1981-2000
% of Workforce in 2009[16]	4%	40%	33%	23%
Projected % of Workforce in 2015[17]	2%	28%	25%	45%
Work Ethic/ Values[18]	Hard work, respect authority, sacrifice	Workaholics, crusading causes, personal fulfillment	Self-reliance, want structure and direction	Multitasking, tenacity, entrepreneurial, goal oriented
Work is...	An obligation	An exciting adventure	A difficult challenge, contract	A means to an end of fulfillment
Messages that Motivate[18]	Your experience is respected	You are valued and needed	Do it your way, never mind the rules	You will work with other bright, creative people. You can do it

Five Strategies for Engaging Millennials

Millennials work a little differently than the current workforce and respond better to certain types of communication. Use these five strategies that are key to their engagement.

1. **Start strong.** Studies suggest that Millennial workers decide on the first day whether they will stay with an organization long-term. Engage them at the beginning with a solid understanding of the organization by sharing its history, mission, vision, and values. If Millennials believe in the company and feel aligned with its mission, they will feel instantly connected.

2. **Encourage and foster creativity.** Millennials aren't shy about wanting an interesting, dynamic, creative and above all, fun working environment. They look for workplaces that have creative communication, open working environments, technology, and flexibility.

3. **Make sure they are challenged.** Millennials have high expectations of themselves and aren't afraid to make mistakes as they learn by doing. Giving them the opportunity to build their experience will pay off in increased capability as it shapes the next generation of leaders.

4. **Coach, coach, coach.** Motivated and open to feedback, Millennials are eager to do well and easy to coach. They want to hear from managers often about their progress throughout the course of the month—or even week. If you catch a Millennial regressing, approach that time as an opportunity for learning. They want to know where they can improve to become the star employees they strive to be.

5. **Chart a career path.** Millennials need to know where they fit and where they can advance in the organization. Establish goals and expectations to help them set their sights on career opportunities. Letting Millennials know there is room for them to grow in the organization over time will engage them and help them reach their goals and yours.

Engaging Millennials is all about understanding them, and what makes them tick. The more you know, the more you can leverage their talent and energy.

How to Communicate with Millennials

As with any audience, when communicating with Millennials it helps to put yourself in their shoes to gain a greater understanding of where they're coming from. When you think about the best way to motivate, or messages most likely to resonate, it may help to keep in mind what Millennials often heard from parents as they were growing up:

The sky's the limit! You can do it! Millennials have had a constant flow of positive reinforcement from parents, coaches, and teachers, and look for similar affirmation in the workplace. They don't want to wait for an annual or bi-annual review, but seek feedback as often as possible—even weekly—to support their desire for career-long improvement. Though it can take some time to offer such feedback consistently, responding to this need keeps young employees motivated and engaged.

Tell it straight. Millennials appreciate honesty and want to know the reality of any situation. They can handle tough news, as long as they are given options for growth. This realistic frame of mind helps them develop skills and meet expectations. Open and honest communication builds a foundation of trust with leadership, ultimately enhancing Millennials' commitment to the organization.

Make your own opportunities. Growing up, Millennials were encouraged by their parents to interact with their superiors—to respect them but not fear them. As they interact with senior-level employees, they are learning how to become leaders themselves. Millennials aren't afraid to make mistakes; they learn by doing and want to be challenged to be the best. By engaging directly with respected leaders, they better understand how to become the employees they strive to be.

While Millennials may have different needs and expectations than past generations, their unique attributes and commitment can be beneficial to any organization. Leaders who engage Millennials can gain a dedicated team of new workers who are energized and motivated employees.

Closing the Gap:
Helping Organizations Adapt to Millennials

As each new generation enters the workplace they bring a fresh set of beliefs, values, styles, and preferences. That can be challenging if other employees aren't prepared.

Think about the bell-bottomed free spirits in the 1970s, who clashed immediately with their elder colleagues from the 1950s.

To help smooth the transition of Millennials into organizations filled with Veterans, Boomers, and Gen Xers, try these five steps.

1. **Create a tolerant, high-performance culture.** Set expectations and model behaviors of teamwork, collaboration, and communication to build a culture that welcomes different styles and points of view. Conduct a thorough orientation so that all new employees—Millennials and others—understand the organization and how it works. Create opportunities for team building and interaction that help employees understand each others' needs and work styles, and how they can work together toward common goals.

2. **Help Millennials understand the big picture.** The reality is they are new to the professional workplace and can benefit from knowledge and mentoring. They will adapt more easily into the organization when they understand what is important to their colleagues and why certain systems are in place.

3. **Help older workers understand Millennials.** Reassure established workers that the new employees may act and think differently than they do, but they want to do well and work hard to succeed.

4. **Educate Millennials on how to meet colleagues' expectations.** They need to realize that the better they understand their colleagues, the easier it will be to succeed in their work. Help them understand that although older colleagues may work a little differently than Millennials, all share similar goals such as financial security, purpose in their career, respectful co-workers, and support in the workplace.

5. **Establish mentoring relationships.** Millennials have generally been encouraged and supported throughout their lives and will appreciate similar relationships with work leaders and colleagues. If other generations know that Millennials respect them and want to learn what they know, this can foster positive and productive work relationships.

"If you want happiness for a lifetime—
help the next generation."

– Chinese Proverb

TRY IT TODAY

Consider ways you can harness Millennials' talent and energy by addressing their needs for challenge, growth, and success.

- **What's changing?** If environments are evolving or needs are changing, it's a great place for Millennials to be involved. Tap into their technological savvy by assigning them to help the organization adapt to new technology or business processes.

- **Where is the challenge?** Look for ways to consistently help Millennials stretch and tackle new challenges. They aren't afraid to make mistakes and thrive on opportunities for growth.

- **Who can they learn from?** Establish coaching and mentoring relationships for Millennials on your team to provide the feedback they need and help them understand how to best contribute to the organization.

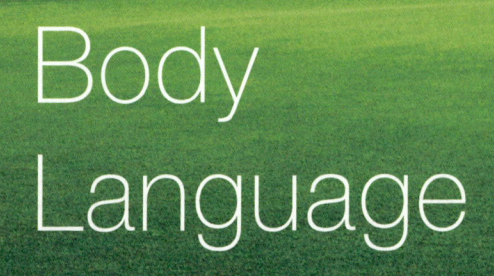

Body
Language

Catching *(and Sending)* Cues That Matter

"Of those who say nothing,
few are silent."

– Thomas Neill, Author

Starting thought

Every-Body Speaks

Body language is something that some of us register and process without even being aware of it, and something that others consistently miss—unaware of the valuable clues to emotions and feelings that body language provides. But no matter where you are on the spectrum of awareness, an enhanced understanding of body language can positively impact your business and interpersonal success.

The basic fact is this: all nonverbal communication has meaning, and body language can be a rich source of information for any leader. Sometimes it's a cue that you aren't connecting, as body language contradicts what's being said; other times, it signals when a message is getting through. In most cases, being sensitive to body language can help us support others and build stronger relationships.

What signals—either intentional or unintentional— might you be sending that help or hinder achievement of your goals?

Body Language Basics That Work

Great leaders know themselves and have an understanding of how others see them. When it comes to body language, where does one begin? With the basics:

Make strong eye contact—Regular eye contact builds relationships and inspires confidence. Looking someone in the eye during a conversation shows respect and interest in what they have to say, while it can seem you are not listening if you avoid eye contact when someone is speaking. If you look away, it can be interpreted as a lack of confidence or give the impression you are lying.

Practice good posture—Stand and sit up straight to show you are relaxed and in command of a situation. Whatever your actual height may be, you will make a positive impression if you stand, walk, and sit tall. Holding your head high indicates open-mindedness and attentiveness. Even if people see you from a distance they will get the message that you are confident and in control.

Use positive expressions—Your facial expressions and body positions are like pictures that paint a thousand words. A smile engages people and promotes positive interaction. Being still, leaning forward and focusing on the person in front of you demonstrate interest and suggest you are open to what they have to say. The opposite impression is given by crossing your arms or legs, hunching shoulders forward, and having a rigid posture. If you are trying to connect with people who present this "closed" position, ask them about themselves or their concerns and listen to what they have to say.

Respect personal space and position—People can become uncomfortable if you encroach on their personal space, which typically ranges between 30 and 36 inches. Consider this when setting chairs for meetings as well as in one-on-one interactions. Also remember seating positions can send a message—placing chairs at a 45-degree angle to one another tends to encourage collaboration, while having a desk or table between people can be a barrier to teamwork.

The Five Truisms of Body Language

1. Your body language communicates all the emotions you feel.

2. What your body communicates to me is more accurate than what you say, and it speaks before you do. People can often tell what you're thinking or feeling before you speak. And your actions can speak so loudly they drown out your words.

3. Employees search a leader's actions for meaning and then act accordingly.

4. Understanding body language can help leaders know when their message resonates and also when more clarification is needed.

5. Different cultures, ages, and genders can assign different meaning to body language, so it is important to consider the types of people involved.

Perfect Practice Makes Perfect, and Other Winning Strategies

Want to improve how you communicate and specifically, the messages you're communicating through your body language? Try these four tried-and-true strategies:

- **Watch others**—Start as a keen observer of others. Watch presenters or leaders you admire and see how they engage others through verbal and nonverbal communication. Note what works and what doesn't.

- **Evaluate yourself**—Use a mirror to watch your facial expressions. Even better, record yourself interacting with others, informally or formally, and decide what changes you may need to make. Watching yourself on videotape is a powerful way to observe yourself in action and note any blind spots you have, or identify signals you're sending that you don't intend.

- **Check with others**—Ask someone you trust if they notice any nonverbal cues that may give the wrong impression.

- **Practice**—Answer questions and make statements in front of the mirror or camera until you are comfortable delivering a sincere message with continuous eye contact.

The Signals You Send

To gain greater awareness of how your body language could be interpreted, videotape and review a rehearsal session for your next big presentation. Evaluate how well your body reinforces your words and consider the signals you may be sending:

- **Self-confidence**—Standing or sitting tall, with shoulders back and head up, making eye contact and smiling, clasping hands behind your back or placing them on your hips.

- **Defensiveness**—Crossed, folded arms, crossed legs with ankles locked, fidgeting.

- **Disagreement or negative response**—Head shaking, head down in response to a speaker, crossed arms, clenched fists, interwoven clenched fingers, pinching of the bridge of the nose, sitting with legs crossed in a figure-4 position.

- **Insecurity**—Standing in "scissor" pose with ankles crossed, sitting with legs intertwined, slouching posture, limited eye contact, keeping head down, gripping your own upper arms.

- **Interest**—Strong eye contact, holding head forward and upright, leaning upper body forward, slow head nodding, leg pointing in the direction of the speaker, sounds of affirmation.

- **Nervousness/tension**—Touching your face, biting your lip, grinding teeth, chewing gum, arm-across-body moves including reaching across for a drink or to adjust clothing, holding an object in front of the body.

- **Thoughtfulness/evaluation**—"Steepling" hands with fingers and thumbs on opposite hands touching, hands stroking chin, pinching or rubbing nose while listening, chin resting on hand with arm on elbow, head tilted to one side.

R-E-S-P-E-C-T

Aretha Franklin had it right. How do you show respect through your body language? Here are some strategies that will be music to your ears; done well, others will take note, too:

Be conscious of body position—Show you are engaged by facing your feet and body toward the person who has your attention (turning sideways may seem you are ready to exit at the first opportunity). Leaning into the conversation shows interest.

Ignore distractions—Pay close attention to a conversation despite distractions. This sends a clear message that the person you are talking to—rather than ringing phones or other interruptions—is your priority.

Establish your presence—Standing upright with legs straight and together is a respectful posture. When you enter a room, you convey a professional presence by observing the environment first before approaching the people you want to speak with.

Make eye contact—This is a first step in getting a person's attention and an important part of active listening. Looking people in the eye shows self-confidence and interest in what they are saying. Be sure to make eye contact when meeting people for the first time and when saying goodbye.

Be still—When you are engaged in conversation, be conscious of body movement that may make you seem nervous, impatient or distracted. Being still shows you are focused on the people you are with and what they are saying.

TIP:

Common denominators

You can be confident in interpreting one of the six facial expressions identified as common across all cultures:

- Happiness
- Sadness
- Fear
- Disgust
- Surprise
- Anger

Be Aware of Cultural Differences

Gestures you use every day can mean very different things to people from other cultures:

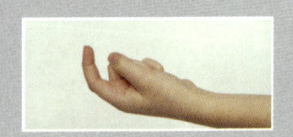

Motion with an index finger—Gesturing for someone to come to you with an index finger is considered rude in many countries, as is pointing. It's better to use an open hand with palm down.

Nodding the head—Moving your head up and down signals affirmation in the United Sates, but it means "no" in Bulgaria and Greece.

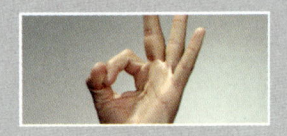

"OK" sign—Creating a circle with thumb and index-finger is a rude gesture in Latin America, Germany, and the Middle East.

V sign with two fingers—With palm outward, this typically means "peace" or "victory" in various cultures, but with the palm facing inward it is offensive in Britain.

Showing soles of the feet/shoes—This is considered insulting in some Eastern countries.

Thumbs up—This positive gesture in Western cultures is considered rude in some Eastern cultures.

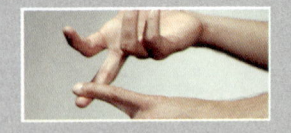

Using the left hand—Not done in Eastern cultures because it is associated with toilet functions, best to use the right hand for everything in Eastern environments.

TRY IT TODAY

Evaluate your understanding of body language and find ways to improve it—as sender and receiver.

• **What signals are you sending?** Ask a trusted friend, family member, or colleague what they notice about your body language that you might not realize, or videotape yourself making a presentation or conducting a meeting. Pay special attention to body language related to respect and interpersonal relationships. Consider corrective measures based on what you learn.

• **How well can you read others' body language?** Observe others as they interact and see what you can infer from their actions and movements. Check with them to see if you've interpreted correctly with a clarifying question such as, "You seem to have a reaction to what I said, what are your thoughts?" Or, describe what you see: "Your brow looks furrowed."

Connecting with Hard-to-Reach Employees

Going the Distance to Engage Them

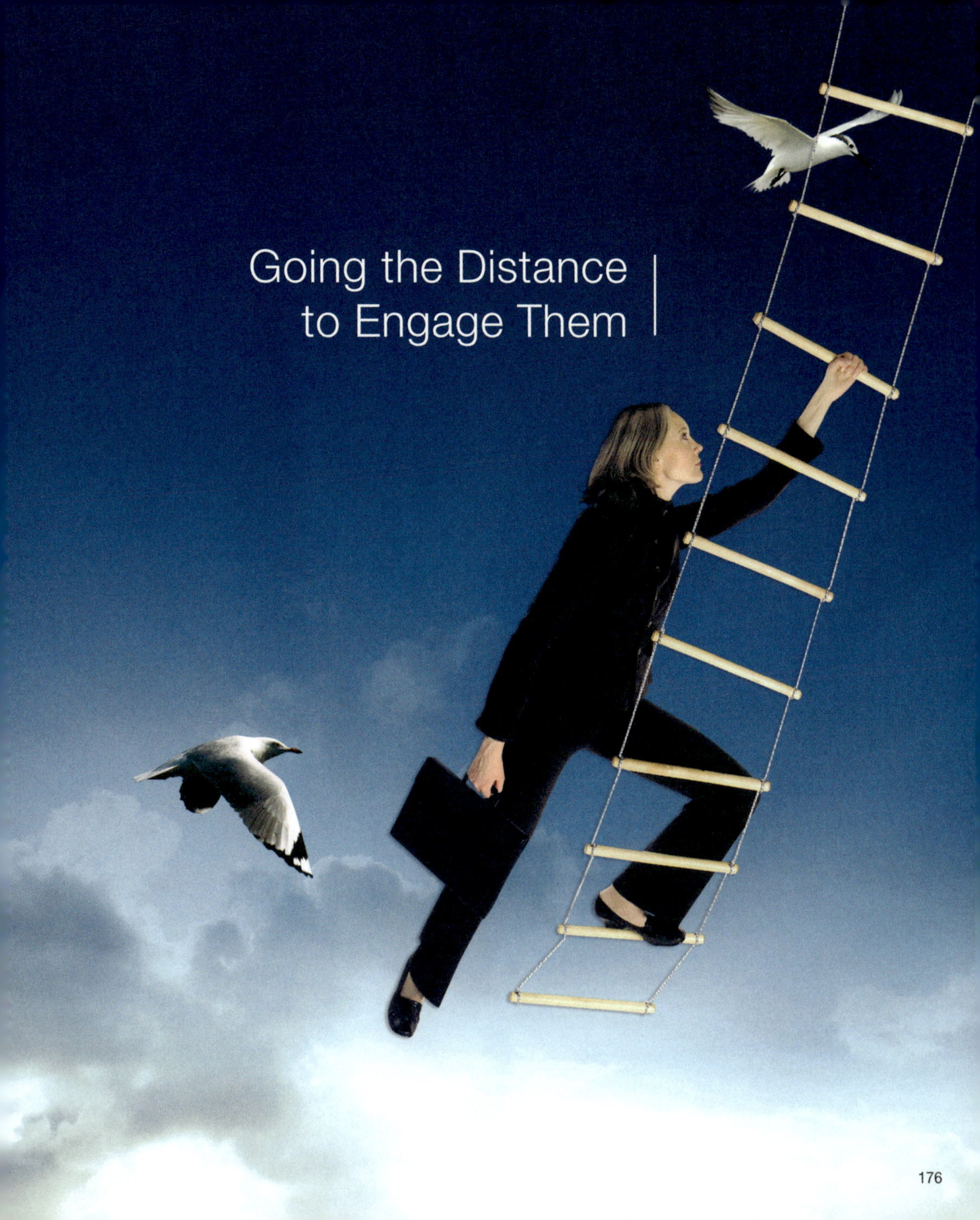

"Creativity is the power to connect the seemingly unconnected."

– William Plomer, Writer

Starting thought

Breaking Through the Hard-to-Reach Barrier

In this world where so many of us are connected 24/7 through technology, there are still many employees who—believe it or not—are hard to reach.

I'm talking about people who have limited face-to-face visibility with senior leaders, or even with their supervisors, and those who are not effectively reached by traditional communication channels.

Hard-to-reach employees may be working in remote offices, constantly on-the-move away from their home base, or on a production floor without phone or e-mail access. They may be part of a global organization that has team members literally in different worlds—across various continents, cultures, and time zones. Some may work virtually and never see their boss face-to-face, even after months on the job.

I saw a real-world example while conducting a client focus group in Europe recently. Several members of the group had never met their bosses face-to-face, but only seen their photos on the intranet. Imagine not being able to recognize your supervisor if they passed you in the hallway! Wherever hard-to-reach employees work and whatever they do, they have something in common: specific needs that require a different approach to communication. Whether we are dealing with technology, translation, time zones, or just plain human nature, leaders need to go beyond the tried-and-true methods to make these employees feel valued and motivated.

Like any communication challenge, connecting with hard-to-reach employees starts with knowing your audience, then understanding how they want to get information.

- What is important to them and how is it best communicated?
- What attracts their attention and what doesn't?
- How can you help connect the dots between their work and the company's goals?

With numbers of hard-to-reach employees growing, and communication a critical part of a supervisor's job, leaders need to ask some critical questions to be sure resources are applied where they should be.

> How well are your supervisors prepared to communicate with hard-to-reach employees?

Is Anybody Out There?
Overcoming *'out of sight, out of mind'* for remote workers

As much as they may appreciate the convenience it offers, people who work remotely can feel far removed from their colleagues in the office. They still need the human connection, conversation, and insight of the workplace even when they are miles away or on the shop floor away from executive offices. Leaders can help remote workers overcome this sense of isolation by including them in the activity of the workplace whenever possible. Be advised that it can take extra effort to get past the day-to-day distractions that command immediate attention in the office.

Here are some tips for helping remote workers feel included and valued:

Communicate predictably
Set regular meeting times and agree on how the team will interact outside the meetings. This lets remote workers know when to expect feedback and how best to follow-up with colleagues and leaders. Should they anticipate a response within two hours, an afternoon, a full day? What methods are acceptable to follow up if something is urgent? Weekly conference calls, web meetings or status reports are management techniques that can work well with remote workers.

Define goals carefully
Setting clear project goals, expectations, and daily and weekly deadlines will help remote employees feel a sense of accomplishment even if they can't connect with a leader for immediate feedback. It also allows for interaction and recognition when milestones are met.

Respond quickly
An afternoon can seem like an eternity to a remote worker who is waiting for your input or response but can't see that you are busy or in an all-day meeting. Even a quick email acknowledgement saying when you can respond is helpful. Consider sharing your daily calendar with employees so they see when you're in meetings or out of the office.

Appreciate frequently
The little things mean a lot to an employee who has few interactions with their manager and other colleagues. Show appreciation for good work and notice when remote employees deliver what you need or respond quickly. Make a special point of acknowledging behavior that you want to encourage, such as accountability, customer service, or responsiveness.

The Upward Trend in Remote Workers

The number of people who work remotely in the U.S. has risen dramatically in recent years and continues to increase.

A study by the WorldAtWork global human resources association estimated that 33.7 million Americans telecommuted at least once a month in 2008, an increase of 43 percent in just five years. Some other highlights:

- There were 17.2 million employee telecommuters in the United States in 2008, an increase of 39 percent from 2006.

- The sum of all teleworkers—33.7 million employees, contractors, and business owners in 2008—grew 17 percent in just two years.

- The most common locations for remote work are home (87 percent), a customer's place of business (41 percent), and car (37 percent)[19].

How to Manage a Virtual Team

When your virtual team is challenged by:	Take the opportunity to:
Communication vs. connection	• Encourage informal interaction to help team members get acquainted • Have different team members present reports each month • Recognize people when they have special projects, heavy workloads or personal news to share
Face-to-face communication	• Use Web meetings and video conferences • Celebrate success together as often as possible, even if not in person
Expectations and roles	• Clearly define individual roles and responsibilities in the context of the overall goal • Brief all team members on roles, expectations, procedures and timeframes needed for success • Regularly reinforce messages around expectations and roles to ensure accountability
Efficient processes and protocols	• Involve teams in developing processes and suggesting protocols that would work best for them • Continually ask for feedback on how processes and protocols are working so they can be changed or updated as necessary
Sharing documents	• Use SharePoint and other file-sharing sites • Post information on intranets • Use consistent time and date stamps so your team manages version control
Miscommunication/ cultural differences	• Establish and agree on common terminology and expectations • Clarify understanding frequently: "When you say X, what do you mean?"
Lack of visibility in the organization	• Celebrate success and include remote workers in team recognition (ensure they see/know you're promoting their successes upward in the organization)
Time zones	• Establish protocols for group meetings that cross time zones • Rotate meeting times in fairness to all
Translation	• Plan/budget for local translation of important global communication

Connect with the Big Picture

Hard-to-reach employees tend to identify more with their business unit or location than the culture and mission of the larger organization. Still, like all employees, to feel like they're making a difference; employees need to make the connection between their work and the larger goals and purpose of the organization.

Here are some ways leaders can help employees feel part of the culture, even from a distance:

Plan your communication to connect business goals at multiple levels of the organization—Communicate strategically so all employees understand the goals and see how their team and individual efforts support them. That means creating key messages for each important communication that link global, country, business unit, and work group goals together, and delivering them consistently to all levels and geographies. Carefully consider the best ways to bring the message to hard-to-reach audiences, which are likely to need a different approach than other employees.

Spend time on vision, mission, and values—Make a point of having this important conversation with remote or non-wired workers. All employees need to know the organization's purpose and aspirations, and embrace the values that guide it. When you make a key decision, tie your logic to one of your strategic goals or values. That reinforces their importance and helps create a sense of cohesiveness among all employees, no matter where they work or what they do.

Specify and model expected behaviors—Clearly state your expectations that employees' behaviors align with the organization's values. Most important, show them how it's done. Modeling specific behaviors around values such as accountability, collaboration, respect, and customer service helps to operationalize them. Be sure to apply rules uniformly to everyone, whether they are working remotely, in the office, or on the shop floor.

Tell compelling stories—Bring the organization's vision to life with stories that recognize successes and highlight desired employee behavior, including that of hard-to-reach workers. Share the stories in virtual or face-to-face group meetings, as well as in other internal communications, to help these employees feel part of the team. Reward them with the chance to present their own successes to colleagues.

Provide context for news and performance updates—Share company news to help people feel connected with the larger organization. Just as important, help people understand the local impact and how employees' work relates directly to the organization's performance.

TIP:

Supervisors: The answer to our prayers?

When it comes to hard-to-reach employees, how much responsibility can we (or should we) reasonably place on supervisors' shoulders?

Consider what we know:

1. Many of the traditional communication channels used aren't as effective for employees in manufacturing plants, for example, or for remote workers. Access and reach often are the barriers.

2. The immediate supervisor is the best and most valued resource for job-related information, according to a myriad of research surveys, including our own work.

3. Even in times of uncertainty, when many questions can't be easily answered and skepticism is high, employees still trust their supervisors most.

4. In general, employees value their supervisors and typically rate them highly in surveys.

Are supervisors the primary answer to the hard-to-reach challenge (of course supplemented by a few other vehicles)? If so, we need to:

- Set expectations on the supervisors' role and hold supervisors accountable in a meaningful way for communication

- Train supervisors in this learned skill called communication

- Provide supervisors the tools they need to succeed

- Measure their progress and celebrate their successes

This just might be a super way to engage those hard-to-reach employees, and where leaders should spend their time, energy, and bucks.

Tips for Reaching Non-Wired Employees

We know that supervisors are critical to communication, but nowhere are they more pivotal to its success than in reaching non-wired employees.

Drivers, manufacturing workers, transportation personnel—anyone whose job has limited need for communication technology—present a particular challenge. In many cases, these people are on the move. They may be on wheels or in the air, traveling from point A to point B, with a job that demands utmost concentration and little connectivity. They may be hourly workers who literally lose money if they take shift time to stop and "receive" communication. They may have some access—maybe to a computer kiosk or remote log-in from home—but often it is limited. Or, they may be part of the shrinking population without the skill to use or access technology.

There are some tried and true methods to reach these special groups:

Posters and signage—Simple and functional signage in manufacturing areas, break rooms, and in locker areas can be effective for non-wired audiences. Use clear language and graphics that reflect the urgency and importance of the information. If material has a short lifespan, note a "remove" date on each item so postings can be kept current.

Shift meetings—Many facilities, from manufacturers to hotels, have a daily stand-up meeting where supervisors share key information and motivational messages and invite employee input. These 5-to-10-minute gatherings must be focused (ideally scripted) to deliver the main talking points. The meetings should follow standards set by the group and take extra time for critical discussions when needed.

Technology kiosks and home access—Even when offered access to technology, these workers may be challenged to use it for any length of time. For people less familiar with technology, placing instruction cards for using certain programs can be helpful. Even for those who are comfortable with technology and access it away from work, less communication is preferable unless they can take work time to read and answer it.

Audio messages—Opportunities to play audio in the workplace, hear it on the intranet, or receive voicemail messages allow for a different communication approach. Brief scripts for key information can include an introduction, call to action, and conclusion.

Text messages—For workers who are highly mobile, group text messaging could be an answer to delivering urgent or critical communication. If it is used across the company, be aware of employee costs involved with receiving text messages and if this becomes a consistent way of communicating, consider covering their work-related expense.

Employee input—Every organization needs one or more ways to gather employees' input so they know their voices are heard. This could include employee surveys, a suggestion box or website form, or even occasional focus groups.

Supervisor support—Employees hear the message when it is repeated often, and educating supervisors in communication can pay big dividends. Be sure to provide them with talking points and tips for major initiatives to help supervisors internalize and share the key information with their employees.

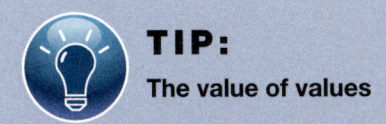

TIP:
The value of values

When you consistently communicate values, people listen. Values are the core of an organization's culture—they help connect even the most diverse and distant employees. Consistent, integrated communication is one of the best ways to achieve alignment around values.

Like other things that are important to the organization, **values must be talked about regularly and integrated into all essential communications**. Hard-to-reach workers, as well as people in the next room or on the shop floor, need to hear leaders reinforce the meaning and importance of

the values they hold dear. They need to see values referenced on the company intranet, in internal newsletters, and in presentations about key initiatives. Even people profiles can highlight values by spotlighting individual successes and challenges.

In the end, it's all about connecting the dots for employees. Values give us the rationale to make decisions. Employees at all levels, including those in hard-to-reach locations, need to know that company decisions are linked to shared values, especially during major organizational change.

Leadership is a Two-Way Street

Leading virtual teams requires more than just presence and project management skills. It means engaging employees who are not in your space and ensuring they feel connected and valued by the organization.

Some key things to remember:

Employees want visible leaders who listen—They want to know their voices are heard, whether they work remotely or not.

Two-way communication is more critical than ever with a distributed, hard-to-reach workforce—Be sure to ask for input and check direction once in a while to be sure everyone has a common understanding of the goals and focus. Don't assume that silence means there is nothing to be said—or heard.

Everyone matters—Ensure everyone participates and is heard during virtual team meetings, either through prepared presentation or spontaneous discussion. If people aren't volunteering information in a virtual meeting, ask them what they think about a topic or invite them to share what they've been doing.

Technology can be a barrier to engagement—Especially when connections are slow or equipment isn't working well, remote workers can become frustrated trying to follow along and participate at the same time they are trying to work out technical issues. Be sensitive to these technological barriers and the learning curve for people using a new technology or system for the first time. Be patient and recognize they may not be as adept at following along as their more experienced peers.

TIP:

What non-wired employees want when it comes to communication

- Fewer and shorter messages
- Clear priorities and direction
- Action-oriented information
- High visibility material
- Signs that get to the point
- Easy access to information
- Local language

TRY IT TODAY

Evaluate your workplace and determine which individuals may benefit from a different approach to your communication:

- **How often do you connect directly with remote workers?** Have you had the chance to get to know them and their needs? Pick and implement two more ways you will try to work better with these employees.

- **When did you last measure employee engagement?** What were the results, and how are you addressing employees' needs?

- **What strategies do you use specifically for non-wired employees?**

- **Where do you see opportunities to do better?** Choose one large and one small activity to take action on in this area.

Closing Thought

Knowing How to Communicate Is Only The First Step

"Things do not change;
we change."

– Henry David Thoreau, Philosopher

There's nothing as invigorating or energizing for me as spending time with clients working on some of their toughest communication challenges. I recently spent time training leaders on two-way communication with a focus on how to plan any kind of communication, as well as the six ultimate interpersonal skills needed for a productive and successful interaction.

The day was filled with education, lots of interaction, and significant chunks of time dedicated to practicing the critical skills. I celebrated with these leaders as they connected the dots and saw immediate application for what we covered, and I felt their frustration when the perfect moment for empathy during a role play turned into a lecture of a valued employee.

At one point during a role play an exasperated leader said to me, "This feels awkward. I know how to do this!"

Two authentic and emotionally self-aware statements.

"Yes," I said, "Exactly. That means you're stepping outside your comfort zone and trying something new. Good for you!"

It gets easier the more you do it.

"This feels awkward."—I was reminded about the discomfort that accompanies real change. Inherent in that discomfort is growth, opportunity, and possibility. True for development opportunities, or the kind of change that is thrust upon us.

Discomfort is a cue that we're growing and developing.

"I know how to do this."—It's one thing to know how to do something; it's another to take that knowledge and apply it, especially in varying situations or times of great change.

A friend of mine is working on shedding some pounds. It's a weighty challenge, even he'll acknowledge *(forgive the pun)*. He's read every book and can describe a ton of strategies that work. That said, he's struggling to put those strategies into practice. He's not alone. While knowledge is power, or empowerment, it's putting that knowledge into action that matters most. **Easier said than done**.

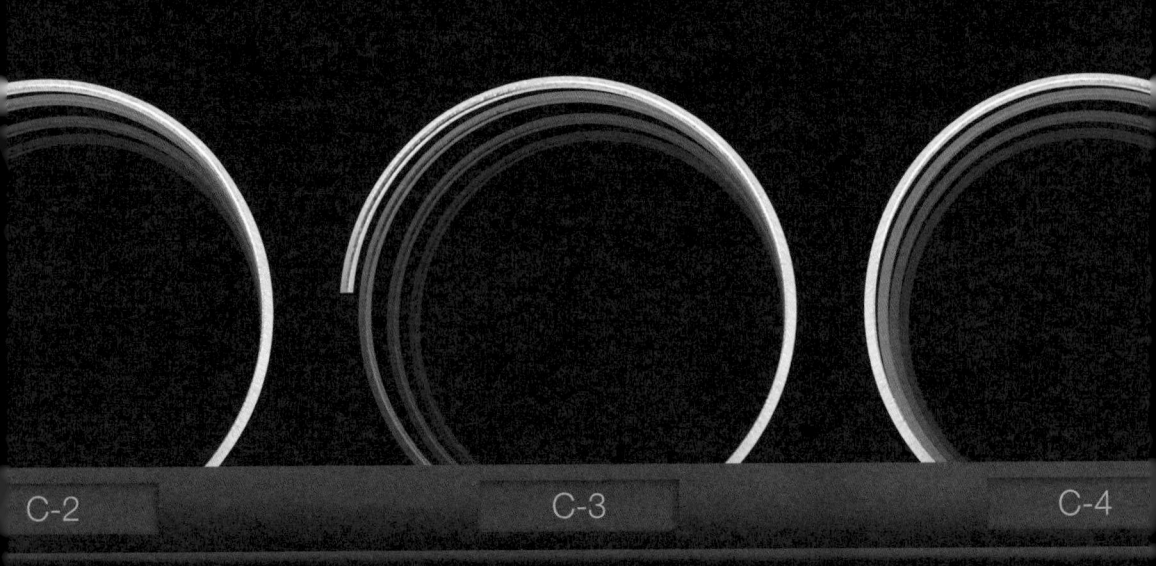

As leaders, we can take charge of change, or we can let change happen to us. We can view change as bad and negative, or as an opportunity. We can fight it, or embrace the learning and development opportunities inherent in every change.

When I worked on the corporate side, I recall being distraught when a key player on my team moved on to a new position. As only time would reveal, the replacement was stronger and even more competent than his predecessor. As the change was happening, I never could have imagined that possibility. I was lost in the "Valley of Despair" and couldn't see the forest for the trees.

In the end, the change was one of the best things that could have happened at the time for me, my team, and for the organization (not to mention for the person who moved on).

B-5 B-6

C-5 C-6

The Tony award-winning musical, **Caroline, or Change**, chronicles the relationship between an African-American maid and a Jewish family right after the assassination of President Kennedy. It's a story of how relationships and life evolve in often unexpected ways. In one scene, Caroline shares this tidbit of wisdom that encapsulates the message of the show: "For change come fast and change come slow, but everything changes…"

In other words, change "*is*."

"Change is inevitable— except from a vending machine."

– *Robert C. Gallagher, Author*

I'm fortunate to regularly spend time on the island of Kauai, one of my most favorite spots in the world. It's also the wettest spot on earth, and I'm used to the frequent and often short-lived rains.

Many tourists are annoyed by the rain; others understand it's the rain that makes the north side of the island incredibly verdant and lush. It also makes for the most beautiful rainbows I've ever seen. Sometimes even double or triple rainbows.

I'll end where I began the book, with the wisdom of Maya Angelou. "There's a rainbow in every cloud. The light is always there. It's yours to seek and find."

May you have great success turning your clouds into rainbows.

1. Harvard Business Review, "What Only The CEO Can Do" (May 2009)

2. LCWA Research Group, "Comparative data from Communication Climate Indices" (2004-2009)

3. Maritz Research, "Managing in an Era of Mistrust" (2010)

4. Internal IBM Branding Study (2010)

5. Franklin Covey, "Less Than Half of U.S. Workers Know or are Committed to Their Organization's Goals" (March 2004)

6. Towers Watson, "Communication ROI Study" (2009/2010)

7. Annals of Internal Medicine, "What Distinguishes Top-Performing Hospitals in Acute Myocardial Infarction Mortality Rates? A Qualitative Study" (March 2011)

8. *New York Times*, "What Makes a Hospital Great" (March 2011)

9. Towers Watson, "Capitalizing on Effective Communication" (2009/2010)

10. Gallup Management Journal, "The Power of Praise and Recognition" (July 2004)

11. James Harter and Rodd Wagner, "12: The Elements of Great Managing" (2007)

12. Zogby Interactive, "U.S. Public Widely Distrusts Its Leaders," Press Release (May 2006)

13. Ralph E. Kenyon Jr., Think-Feel and Know-Act, 1979

14. Strategic HR Review, "The Three Dimensions of Engagement," Volume 4 Issue 2 (2005)

15. BNET, "What is a millennial?" (2008)

16. Bureau of Labor Statistics, "Household Data Annual Averages," (2009)

17. Harvard Business Review, "Are You Ready to Manage Five Generations of Workers?" (2009)

18. FDU Magazine Online, "Mixing and Managing Four Generations of Employees," (2005)

19. WorldatWork and Dieringer Research Group, "Telework Trendlines" (2009)

Would you like David to present a powerful program to your organization?

David Grossman is a much sought-after speaker and consultant, acclaimed for his highly engaging, interactive, and powerful programs. He's known for his thoughtful, personal, and pragmatic approach that leverages communication as one of the ultimate business tools.

From Fortune 100 companies to professional associations and universities, David's proven leadership communication programs benefit leaders at all levels and help them connect the dots between communication and business results.

To request a speaker's kit or for more information, please visit: www.yourthoughtpartner.com/speaking-and-events

?

Give Us Feedback on *You Can't Not Communicate 2*

We're interested in what you think. What was most helpful? Least helpful?

What's working for you that we should share with others?

What new challenges do you face today?

E-mail us your thoughts at **results@yourthoughtpartner.com.**

David Grossman

ABC, APR, Fellow PRSA, is both a student and teacher of effective communication. He is one of America's foremost authorities on communication inside organizations.

Known for his thoughtful, personal, and pragmatic approach, David coaches leaders at all levels to utilize communication as a strategic business tool. The "anti-social media guy," David addresses both the importance of effective internal and leadership communication and the critical need for face-to-face communication amid the surge of electronic media. By acting as an advocate for employees and a **thought**partner to senior management, David and his team help organizations unleash the power of communication to engage employees and drive performance.

Leveraging his background in organizational development and psychology, David also facilitates training programs developed exclusively for senior leadership teams at Fortune 500 companies and other leading organizations. David also answers leadership and employee communication questions everyday through his "Ask David" iPhone application.

His first book, *"You Can't NOT Communicate: Proven Communication Solutions That Power the Fortune 100"* has received accolades and praise from leaders, communication professionals, and educators for "reminding leaders (everywhere and at all levels) of the importance of getting communication right" and for providing "proven and practical insights, methods, and tools" to enhance results and ensure overall engagement.

David currently teaches the only graduate-level course in internal communications in the U.S. at Columbia University. He has been published in numerous industry journals and is the author of *"Internal Branding: How to Create and Sustain a Successful Internal Brand," "The Practitioner's Guide to Essential Techniques for Employee Engagement,"* and the CD-ROM *"messagemaps: A Guide to Creating Clear, Credible and Impactful Messages."*

David was recently named to *USA Today's* corporate management and leadership CEO panel. In 2009, he was a finalist for the NGLCC Wells Fargo Business Owner of the Year Award, honoring his entrepreneurial spirit for business performance, innovation, growth, and personal service to the community. He is a member of the National Speakers Association and is a designated IABC recommended speaker.

Prior to founding The Grossman Group in 2000, David was director of communications for McDonald's. David graduated summa cum laude, Phi Beta Kappa from the University of Wisconsin-Madison with an honors degree in journalism and holds a master's in Corporate Public Relations from Northwestern University. He began his career as a journalist, working in radio news and television.

THE
GROSSMAN
GROUP

About The Grossman Group

Twice named *PR Week's* "Boutique Agency of the Year" and *The Holmes Report's* "Employee Communication Agency of the Year," The Grossman Group (www.yourthoughtpartner.com) is an award-winning Chicago-based communications consultancy focusing on organizational consulting, strategic leadership development, and internal communications.

The Grossman Group's client roster includes Fortune 500 clients such as Accor, Cisco, Heinz, Intel, LifeScan, Lilly, Lockheed Martin, McDonald's, Microsoft, Rockwell Automation, UNUM and Virgin Atlantic.

Using its unique Grossman Methodology—encompassing its award-winning proprietary tools, training and **thought**partner approach—the consultancy delivers proven, breakthrough strategies that solve clients' business challenges, especially around:

- Minimizing the downside of change when business could be interrupted, slowed, or stopped

- Turning employee confusion, skepticism, and apathy into productivity and engagement

- Maximizing the upside of change to accelerate business results

The Grossman Group is a certified diversity supplier through the National Gay and Lesbian Chamber of Commerce (NGLCC). In 2010, The Grossman Group was named by DiversityBusiness.com as one of the top 500 diversity-owned businesses in the U.S. The Grossman Group's work has won all the "Oscars" of communications—the prestigious Silver Anvil Award from the Public Relations Society of America (PRSA), the Gold Quill Award from the International Association of Business Communicators (IABC), the Golden World Award from the International Public Relations Association (IPRA), and SABRE Awards from The Holmes Report.

Be Connected

Visit Our Website

Go to www.yourthoughtpartner.com to learn more about The Grossman Group and its proven approach to strategic leadership and internal communication. Also download free eBooks such as *"The Greatest Mistakes (you don't want to make)"* and *"The Top 5 Reasons **(Excuses)!** We're So Bad at Communicating."*

Subscribe to ethoughtstarters

For quick, simple tips to help build better leader**communicators** subscribe to our **e**thought**starters** newsletter by visiting www.yourthoughtpartner.com/ethought-starters.

Participate in the Discussion

To see what others are saying on the latest topics and issues around communication and to post your own thoughts, check out David's blog at www.yourthoughtpartner.com/blog. You can also engage on LinkedIn and through David's **"Ask David"** app for iPhone and Droid.

Get Quantity Discounts

Books are available at quantity discounts on orders of 50 copies or more. Please call us at 312.829.3252, visit us online at www.yourthoughtpartner.com/you-cant-not-communicate-2 or email office@yourthoughtpartner.com.

Invite David to Speak

To help your leaders at all levels be better communicators, invite David to speak to groups large and small by going to www.yourthoughtpartner.com/speaking-and-events.

Stay Connected

Thousands of readers continue to receive communication tools and best practices from David. You can do so too, by subscribing to the leader**communicator blog** or by following David on Twitter at **@ThoughtPartner**.